FROM A DROP OF WATER

From a Drop of Water

A Collection of Magickal Reflections on
the Nature, Creatures, Uses, and Symbolism of Water

Edited by
Kim Huggens

Published by Avalonia

Published by Avalonia

BM Avalonia
London
WC1N 3XX
England, UK

www.avaloniabooks.co.uk

FROM A DROP OF WATER
Copyright © Kim Huggens 2009
Individual authors and artists retain the copyright to their original work.

ISBN-10: 1-905297-34-3
ISBN-13: 978-1-905297-34-4

First Edition, December 2009
Design by Satori

Cover Image "Dark Mother" by Nina Falaise (c) 2009

British Library Cataloguing in Publication Data. A catalogue record for this book is available from the British Library

All rights reserved. No part of this publication may be reproduced or utilized in any form or by any means, electronic or mechanical, including photocopying, microfilm, recording, or by any information storage and retrieval system, or used in another book, without written permission from the authors.

Other Books by Avalonia

A Collection of Magical Secrets Edited by S Skinner, D Rankine

Artemis – Virgin Goddess of the Sun & Moon by Sorita d'Este

Both Sides of Heaven Edited by Sorita d'Este, Various Contributors

Circle of Fire by Sorita d'Este and David Rankine

Climbing the Tree of Life by David Rankine

Defences Against the Witches Craft by John Canard

From a Drop of Water Edited by Kim Huggens, Various Contributors

Heka Ancient Egyptian Magic & Ritual By David Rankine

Hekate Keys to the Crossroads Edited by Sorita d'Este, Various

Hekate Liminal Rites by Sorita d'Este and David Rankine

Horns of Power Edited by Sorita d'Este, Various Contributors

Odin's Gateways by Katie Gerrard

Practical Elemental Magick by Sorita d'Este and David Rankine

Practical Planetary Magick by Sorita d'Este and David Rankine

Practical Qabalah Magick by Sorita d'Este and David Rankine

Priestesses Pythonesses & Sibyls Edited by Sorita d'Este, Various

The Book of Treasure Spirits Edited by David Rankine

The Divine Struggle by Frederic Lamond

The Guises of the Morrigan by Sorita d'Este and David Rankine

The Isles of the Many Gods by Sorita d'Este and David Rankine

Towards the Wiccan Circle by Sorita d'Este

Visions of the Cailleach by Sorita d'Este and David Rankine

Wicca Magickal Beginnings by Sorita d'Este and David Rankine

Wizardry for the Uninitiated by Thea Faye

These and other esoteric titles are available from:

WWW.AVALONIABOOKS.COM

WWW.AVALONIABOOKS.CO.UK

Avalonia, BM Avalonia, London, WC1N 2XX, UK

Table of Contents

FOREWORD 9
    By Kim Huggens 9

THE CONTRIBUTORS 13

ANAHITA 21
    By Payam Nabarz 21

DANCING WITH WATER 31
    By Nina Falaise 31

THE MIRROR OF THE SOUL 35
    by Yvonne Aburrow 35

MARRIED TO THE SEA 42
    By Chrissy Derbyshire 42

THE ADMIRAL, THE SIREN AND WHALE 47
    By Kim Huggens 47

TO DARE 67
    By Sorita d'Este 67

THE WELL SPRING OF WISDOM 84
    By Katherine Sutherland 84

A FLOW OF WATER THROUGH THE GRIMOIRE WORLD 95
    By Maestro Nestor 95

NIMUE **109**

    BY EMILY CARDING 109

QUENCHING THE THIRST, DRINKING THE SPIRIT **120**

    BY JOHN CANARD 120

THE QUEEN OF THE OCEANS **125**

    BY ANDREA SALGADO REYES 125

MAYANS, MAIZE AND MUCH-NEEDED RAIN **131**

    BY RACHEL DONALDSON 131

A FEAST FOR WATER **135**

    RODNEY ORPHEUS & CATHRYN ORCHARD 135

STRUNG LIKE PEARLS **141**

    by DIANE M. CHAMPIGNY 141

RITUALS OF WATER **149**

    BY MAGIN 149

WATER: A KEY TO HEALING **161**

    BY HARRY BARRON 161

THE MOON **165**

    BY MELISSA HARRINGTON 165

Cover Image "Dark Mother" by Nina Falaise (c) 2009

For more information on her work you can contact Nina by e-mail
leonine.cooper@btinternet.com

FOREWORD

BY KIM HUGGENS

"From a drop of water, a logician could infer the possibility of an Atlantic or a Niagara without having seen or heard of one or the other."
~ A Study in Scarlet, Sir Arthur Conan Doyle.

When I started the initial phase of collecting a series of essays on the magickal nature of water I was unsure what results I would find. As the quote above – which also lends itself to this anthology's title – suggests, the subject of water is manifold and fluid, and from the original suggestion of the term a writer could explore almost any avenue of thought regarding it. The articles that were contributed by the authors beautifully demonstrate this fact, and highlight the ability of water to take on many forms and to have a profound effect on so many areas of our lives.

Many of the articles herein have highlighted the scientific fact of water's importance for the human body and the environment around us, and the necessity of it for the survival of all life on earth. As such, they make us aware that we are completely dependent upon this element of water. From such dependence one might expect a relationship manifesting in a similar way to that of the dependence of the body on food, wherein both a positive and a negative relationship can occur. However, it seems that the fluid nature of water allows us to build a relationship with it in a way that best suits each of us individually, and thus the relationships that grow are overwhelmingly personal, coloured by factors such as immediate environment, gender, occupation, religious and spiritual beliefs, and literary inspiration. Whereas for one individual water may manifest in their life as a strong love of the sea, for another it comes to them as a symbol of lifeblood, and still to another it is representative of the archetypal feminine.

These articles not only demonstrate a variety of relationships with water in its many forms, but also approach the subject from different perspectives and using different methods. Most of them examine the rituals in which water is used and plays a foremost role in, including Magin's *Rituals of Water,* in which she examines how water has been used in ritual contexts throughout the world, and how it has manifested in mythology and spiritual practices. In *A Feast for Water: Baptism in the Thelemic Tradition* authors Rodney Orpheus and Cathryn Orchard specifically examine the use of water in the baptismal rite of the *Ecclesia Gnostica Catholica,* placing it in the context of ancient baptismal rites and the writings of Aleister Crowley. Grimoire magician Maestro Naestor, in *A Flow of Water Through the Grimoire World,* focuses more specifically on the creation and use of holy water and baptism in the medieval grimoires and the beings associated with water in the *Goetia* and similar texts. Katherine Sutherland's article, *The Well Spring of Wisdom: Sacred wells in Faith through the Ages,* explores the customs and religious traditions that have arisen around sacred wells, springs, and spas and the significance this holds for modern magicians. Finally, John Canard has written an essay regarding the use of water in the rituals and practices of British root magick, highlighting the syncretic nature of root magick to absorb useful practices from a wide variety of traditions in much the same way that water acts as a carrier for other substances and absorbs readily other liquids (*Quenching the Thirst, Drinking the Spirit: Water and Water Guardians in Root Magick.*)

Many of the authors have chosen to explore the figures that have arisen around both the element of water and the abstract concepts associated with it. Emily Carding's essay, *Nimue, the Archetypal Priestess,* looks at this figure that we more commonly know as the Lady of the Lake, and the historical development of her character in Arthurian literature as well as her meaning in the modern Pagan movement. Meanwhile Payam Nabarz has contributed an article on *Anahita: Lady of Persia,* in which he tracks the development of her worship through the ancient world and her resurgence in the modern. In *Mayans, Maize and Much-Needed Rain* Rachel Donaldson takes a look at the Mayan deities of rain and water and their role in Mayan society and agriculture. My own article, *The Admiral, the Siren and the Whale: Water Spirits in the Vodou Tradition,* examines a plethora of spirits that are either found in water, personify water, or rule over it in Haitian and 21 Divisions Vodou. Andrea Salgado Reyes has discussed the much-loved spirit from Santeria, Yemanyá, and her personal experiences of her in *The Queen of the Oceans: the Afro-Brazilian Goddess Yemanyá and Sea Magic.* From a literary perspective Diane M.

Champigy, in her article *Strung Like Pearls: Dion Fortune's Sea Priestess and its Relationship to the Elemental Contacts of Water,* has analysed *The Sea Priestess* novel by Dion Fortune, in particular focusing on the character of the Sea Priestess herself, what she represents, and the revelations regarding the nature of the ocean and the souls of humans that the book provides.

In several articles the nature of water and humankind's relationship with it is explored from a specific academic perspective, namely in Yvonne Aburrow's contribution, *The Mirror of the Soul: Assessing the Function of Watery Rituals and Folk Beliefs,* and Chrissy Derbyshire's article, *Married to the Sea: Eroticism in Ocean Lore.* The former is an archaeological analysis of British ritual deposits in water, water spirits of the British Isles, and the significance of this for ancient people; the latter presents a literary and mythological analysis of oceanic lore from simple sea shanties to legends of sirens and mermaids to represent the yearning love of the sea. Harry Barron, in *Water: A Key to Healing,* also explores the nature and significance of water from the perspective of a healer, highlighting its functional properties in the healing process.

The effects of water upon the human body and psyche are looked at by Melissa Harrington in her article *The Moon, the Door of Dreams, and the Tides Within,* and by Nina Falaise in *Dancing with Water.* The former examines the symbolic nature of water and its relation to the individual tides of our psyches, dreamworld and magickal undertakings; the latter presents a beautiful guided meditation in the form of a dance visualisation that encourages the reader to engage with the concepts of flow, joy, life and ebb represented by water.

Despite the manifold approaches to this subject, each of the authors demonstrates some of the recurring themes that can be found regarding water. Water is tangible and sensuous – the rituals associated with it involve touching it, bathing in it, drinking it, and coming into physical contact with it in some way. Water has a profound effect not only on the physical survival and growth of the body but also a psychic and emotional effect that is often keenly felt by human beings, and therefore processed and manifested as folklore, myths, water spirits, and literature. The ever-present nature of water throughout the world provides some common ground within world cultures and religions. Water is such a commonplace occurrence – rain, rivers, lakes, seas, mist, blood, spit, tapwater, drink, tears – that we often take for granted in the Western world but which carries human life from birth to death. It cleanses us, refreshes us, drowns us, nourishes us, cools us, and inspires us. It is variously a lover, a friend, an enemy, a ruler, a symbol, a god, or a tool.

All the various ways in which water manifests on the globe and in our minds, hearts and souls, in our religious practices and our literature, are just individual drops of water in the great ocean of meaning.

    Kim Huggens
    Wales, Autumn 2009

The Contributors

Yvonne Aburrrow

Yvonne Aburrow has been a Pagan since 1985, a Wiccan since 1991, and a Unitarian since 2007. She has completed an MA in Contemporary Religions and Spiritualities at Bath Spa University. She has written four books: *The Enchanted Forest: the magical lore of trees*; *Auguries and Omens: the magical lore of birds*; *The Sacred Grove: the mysteries of the forest*; and *The magical lore of animals*. She lives in Bristol, and is married to Nick Hanks, an archaeologist.

Harry Barron

Harry Barron has been interested in holistic healing from a very early age, and for many years from the mid 1990's he was the chairperson of a charity promoting holistic living. He works as an Acupuncturist with a practice split between the heart of Wales and Birmingham. In addition to his work within the field of healing and charity, he is also the translator of the French manuscripts which forms the core of the highly acclaimed *Veritable Key of Solomon* and *A Collection of Magical Secrets* (Skinner & Rankine). He is currently working on further translations of rare and previously unexplored magickal Grimoires exploring the magic of the psalms and Qabalah. Harry has previous contributed essays to anthologies edited by Sorita d'Este on his personal spiritual path. For more information of his practices and therapies, please go to his blog/web pages, http://healingcymru.blogspot.com and http://eaglegrove.blogspot.com.

John Canard

English Root magician John Canard believes that life is best lived as a magical experience that never ends. He had a misspent youth in the Cambridgeshire fens, then he met the woman of his dreams, whom he still believes to be only part human and with her moved to Somerset to live the wild life. They live on a small farm where John spends his time tending a menagerie of animals and growing organic produce. He has always enjoyed writing. His first book *Defences Against the Witches'*

Craft was published by Avalonia in 2008. He previously also contributed essays to both *Horns of Power* (2008) and *Hekate Keys to the Crossroads* (2006) as well as a number of folklore magazines and journals over the years. He is currently working on a number of other projects related to traditional magick, witchcraft and root cunning.

Emily Carding

Emily Carding is a self-taught artist and author, best known for her Tarot work. Creations include the groundbreaking *Transparent Tarot* and the *Tarot of the Sidhe*. She has recently finished work on the *Transparent Oracle*, a seventy card transparent deck based on the seven directions, which forms circular mandalas when cards are layered. Her work has also featured in magazines and book covers, including Avalonia's *Both Sides of Heaven*, for which she also contributed an essay. She currently has a number of projects on the boil and creative ideas in gestation! For more information, please visit www.childofavalon.com

Diane M. Champigny (Thea)

Thea is a 3rd Degree High Priestess and Lineage Elder of the Alexandrian Tradition of Witchcraft. She is an active member of the Society of Elder Faiths and has served as a Ritualist and Workshop Facilitator for the Wiccan Educational Society, an International Pagan Community. Thea is also a Trance Medium, Occult Bibliophile and contributing author of the book *Priestesses, Pythonesses, Sibyls* published by Avalonia. Inquiries may be directed to PriestessThea@hotmail.com or for more detailed information, visit Thea at http://www.myspace.com/PriestessThea.

Chrissy Derbyshire

Chrissy Derbyshire is an author and teacher living in Cardiff. She has been a keen student of mythology and folklore for many years. Her first collection of poetry and short stories, *Mysteries*, was published in 2008. She has since contributed to *The Raconteur* magazine, and continues to write and study.

Sorita d'Este

Sorita d'Este is an esoteric researcher, author and priestess who brings her knowledge of the wisdom of the ancient world into the modern age. Her particular areas of interest relate to the Western Esoteric Traditions, including the Pagan Gods and Goddesses of Ancient Egypt, Greece, Rome, Celtic Britain and Ireland, folklore, Qabalah, divinatory and magical practices through the ages. Her published works include *Practical Elemental Magick, Practical Planetary Magick, Visions of the Cailleach* and *Hekate Liminal Rites*. She remains actively involved in the Western Esoteric Tradition, with a focus on the Greco-Egyptian mysteries and rituals as presented in grimoires such as the *Key of Solomon*. For more information visit www.sorita.co.uk

Rachel Donaldson

Rachel has had a love affair with all aspects of nature for as far as she can remember. As a teen she spent a lot of time hiking throughout the UK. The energies she encountered in remote places led her to spiritual questions that have been slowly answered over the years through yoga, Wicca and more recently shamanism. Hiking still has a place in her life and is all the more enriched through her spiritual experiences. Rachel lives in Kent with her partner.

Nina Falaise

Nina Falaise was born into a theatrical family in July 1955 in Skipton, Yorkshire. When she was a few months old her parents moved to London were she spent most of her early childhood. It was not until Nina was three years old that the doctors discovered she was profoundly deaf. Despite her hearing impairment, Nina trained as a ballet dancer and at sixteen was invited to join her first ballet company. She travelled extensively with touring dance companies all through her teens and early twenties. While on a contracted job with the Balletto di Roma she met her first husband and eventually had two beautiful daughters, Tanja and Natasha. Now, Nina lives in Great Malvern with her second husband Paul Leo, Percy, their adorable Springer Spaniel, and Paul Leo's beautiful children on weekends.

Nina has been an active participant in the Western Mystery tradition for many years, contributing her experience of dance and choreography to ceremonial ritual magic and sacred dance/dramas.

She is also a Visionary artist who is inspired through ritual, meditation work and her ongoing studies of the Great Work. She has several artistic projects on the go, and has recently started working on a project with Paul Leo, which involves painting images for a hundred numerology cards. For workshops and art work by Nina contact leonine.cooper@btinternet.com

Melissa Harrington

Melissa Harrington is a freelance author, Wiccan High Priestess, and initiate and teacher of the Western Mystery Tradition. She is frequently invited to speak at conferences in the magical, occult and Pagan communities. Her particular interests are in mapping the Pagan revival, including its foundation myths, and understanding the psychological and sociological basis of contemporary Pagan religion. Melissa's researches in her chosen field of expertise led her to undertake a degree in psychology, followed by a PhD in Theology and Religious studies at Kings College, focussing on Wicca. Since then she has contributed chapters to some of the leading academic literature in Pagan studies. As a magician Melissa is fascinated with the technology of ritual, and its effect on the human psyche, and she continues to practise diverse magical arts; from rising on the aires of Enochian magic, to working with the Otherworld of fairy lore, with her husband and magical companions. As a continuation of her magical path Melissa is currently studying Yoga and Tai Chi, and she hopes to combine them with contemporary Western ritual form in a further development of her Craft. Melissa's main focus in life is being a full time Mum, which she sees as the most magical and rewarding endeavour she has ever been honoured to undertake.

Kim Huggens

Kim Huggens is currently undertaking her PhD research in the Ancient History department of Cardiff University, looking at the malefic-erotic magic of the Late Antique period. She is a Tarot reader of 16 years experience, and co-creator of *Sol Invictus: The God Tarot* with Nic Phillips (Schiffer Books, 2007.) She has a homestudy Tarot book forthcoming with Llewellyn publications (Spring 2010) and also writes articles and papers for various anthologies and journals. Previous work has appeared in *Horns of Power, The Mithras Reader vol. 2, Priestesses, Pythonesses and Sibyls,* and *Both Sides of Heaven.*

She is a Vodou practitioner and Hounsi Lave Tet with Sosyete Gade Nou Leve, and a member of the Ordo Templi Orientis. In her spare time she creates group ritual, runs Tarot workshops and classes, writes short fiction, and roleplays.

Payam Nabarz

Payam Nabarz is author of *The Mysteries of Mithras: The Pagan Belief That Shaped the Christian World* (Inner Traditions, 2005), *The Persian Mar Nameh: The Zoroastrian Book of the Snake Omens & Calendar* (Twin Serpents, 2006), and *Divine Comedy of Neophyte Corax and Goddess Morrigan* (Web of Wyrd, 2008). He is also the editor of *Mithras Reader An academic and religious journal of Greek, Roman, and Persian Studies.* Volume 1(2006), Volume 2 (2008) and *Stellar Magic: a Practical Guide to Rites of the Moon, Planets, Stars and Constellations* (Avalonia, 2009). For further info visit: www.stellarmagic.co.uk

Maestro Nestor

Maestro Nestor's interest in the occult stemmed from an interest in the darker aspects of magic during his teens, including Satanism, which he practiced until his early twenties. On a trip to New York things changed when during a book buying spree he encountered Cavendish's *The Black Arts* and Waite's *The Book of Black Magic* which introduced him to the grimoire traditions, and since then he has explored the right hand path traditions extensively. His work has previously been published on a variety of websites, as well as in Swedish language magazines. His essay *Demons & Devils* appeared in the *Both Sides of Heaven* anthology edited by Sorita d'Este. He is currently engaged in working on a series of books on the practice of grimoire magic. See www.grimoiremagic.com for more information.

Magin

Magin is a student of the Western magickal tradition and has an academic background in English literature and education policy. She is a Wiccan, a runic practitioner and also works with reiki, intuitive healing and journeying techniques. Magin is a keen painter, gardener, writer, singer, and a DIY enthusiast. She lives in London with her long-suffering partner and their three cats. Magin's artwork features on the cover of the anthology *Hekate Keys to the Crossroads*, to which she also contributed an essay about her experiences with Hekate.

Rodney Orpheus and Cathryn Orchard

Rodney Orpheus has been a member of Ordo Templi Orientis, an international fraternal initiatory magical Order, for 20 years and is a Bishop of its religious arm, the Gnostic Catholic Church. He is the author of *Abrahadabra: Understanding Aleister Crowley's Thelemic Magick* and a well-known writer, musician, lecturer, and broadcaster. Cathryn Orchard joined the Order in 2004 and has recently received ordination as a Priestess of the Church. She works as an Art Psychotherapist and previously contributed to the anthology *Priestesses, Pythonesses & Sibyls*.

Andrea Salgado Reyes

Andrea Salgado Reyes is a Chilean witch and Orixá devotee, blessed by being a daughter of Yemanyá and of Ogún. She has established Comunidad Paganus, a neo-pagan and pagan community in Chile, on a hill within sight of the sea. Her main interests are Wicca, Candomblé and traditional Latin American witchcraft. By profession she is a translator and interpreter. She has previously contributed to *Priestesses, Pythonesses & Sibyls* (Avalonia 2007).

Katherine Sutherland

Katherine Sutherland is an occult scholar and practitioner with wide ranging interests. Also a poet and author of fiction, Katherine is currently working on a children's novel focused on a character not dissimilar to Dr John Dee. Her poetic reworking of the Persephone myth entitled *Underworld* is currently awaiting publication and will be available in 2009. Katherine is a Priestess in the Fellowship of Isis, and a devotee of the flowing spiritual path that her gods have chosen for her. She has previously contributed to *Both Sides of Heaven*.

"This creation is, in its totality, a drop of Water; man himself has originated from a drop of Water"

~ Bundahishn 28,2

GODDESS ANAHITA, PAINTING BY AKASHNATH, 2008

ANAHITA

LADY OF PERSIA

BY PAYAM NABARZ

The following is based on the Anahita chapter from *The Mysteries of Mithras: The Pagan Belief That Shaped the Christian World*. By Payam Nabarz, Inner Traditions, 2005.

> *Mighty Anahita with splendour will shine,*
> *Incarnated as a youthful divine.*
> *Full of charm her beauty she will display,*
> *Her hip with charming belt she will array.*
> *Straight-figured, she is as noble bride,*
> *Freeborn, herself in puckered dress will hide.*
> *Her cloak is all decorated with gold,*
> *With precious dress Anahita we shall behold.*
> (Original poem based on Kashani's Persian folk songs, from an Avestan invocation to Anahita)

Dusk of Shabe Yalda (Yule) 777 BCE, somewhere on a beach by the Caspian sea. A young Magi (who may later known as the prophet Zoroaster) has been keeping a night vigil. His solitary fire is the only light for miles around and his recitation of Aban Yasht - the hymn to angel-goddess Anahita - the only sound to be heard apart from the waves gently crashing onto the beach:

> "Angel-Goddess of all the waters upon the earth and the source of the cosmic ocean; she who drives a chariot pulled by four horses: wind, rain, cloud, and sleet; your symbol is the eight-rayed star. You are the source of life, purifying the seed of all males and the wombs of all females, also cleansing the milk in the breasts of all mothers. Your connection with life means warriors in battle prayed to you for survival and victory.
> A maid, fair of body, most strong, tall-formed, high-girded, pure, . . . wearing a mantle fully embroidered with gold; ever holding the baresma [sacred plant] in your hand, . . . you wear square

golden earrings on your ears . . . a golden necklace around your beautiful neck, . . . Upon your head . . . a golden crown, with a hundred stars, with eight rays . . . with fillets streaming down."[1]

The Magi's prayer is answered by the sea in the form of a vision; as midnight approaches and time slows, the sea parts. A large silver throne appears; on either side of it sits a lion with eyes of blue flame. On the throne sits a Lady in silver and gold garments, proud and tall, an awe-inspiring warrior-woman, as terrifying as she is beautiful. Tall and statuesque she sits, her noble origins evident in her appearance, her haughty authority made clear and commanding through a pair of flashing eyes. A dove flies above her and a peacock walks before her. A crown of shining gold rings her royal temples; bejewelled with eight sunrays and one hundred stars, it holds her lustrous hair back from her beautiful face. Her marble-like white arms reflect moonlight and glisten with moisture. She is clothed with a garment made of thirty beaver skins, and it shines with the full sheen of silver and gold. The planet Venus shines brightly in the sky.[2]

Time passes... history takes place...

Circa 400 BCE Achaemenian king Artaxerxes II Mnemon (404-359 BCE) inscribes in Ecbatana in his palace:

> *"Artaxerxes, the great king, the king of kings, the king of all nations, the king of this world, the son of king* Darius *[II Nothus], Darius the son of king Artaxerxes [I Makrocheir], Artaxerxes the son of king Xerxes, Xerxes the son of king* Darius, *Darius the son of Hystapes, the Achaemenid, says: this hall [apadana] I built, by the grace of Ahuramazda, Anahita, and Mithra. May Ahuramazda, Anahita, and Mithra protect me against evil, and may they never destroy nor damage what I have built."*[3]

Artaxerxes II, like other Achaemenian kings, was initiated by priests at a sanctuary of Anahita in Pasargadai during his coronation. Artaxerxes II built the temple of Anahita at Kangavar near Kermanshah

---

1 From verses 126–128 of the Aban Yasht 5.
2 This description of Anahita is based on her description in Tony Allan, Charles Phillips, and Michael Kerrigan, Myth and Mankind series: Wise Lord of the Sky: Persian Myth (London: Time Life Books, 1999), 32.
3 See: http://www.livius.org/aa-ac/achaemenians/A2Ha.html

as well as many others. The Kangavar was a magnificent temple four-fifths of a mile in circumference, built using cedar or cypress trees. All the columns and floor-tiles were covered with gold and silver. It was perhaps one of the most breathtaking buildings ever built in the Middle East.

Anahita's role as the goddess of water, rain, abundance, blessing, fertility, marriage, love, motherhood, birth, and victory became well established. This goddess was the manifestation of women's perfection. Ancient kings were crowned by their queens in Anahita's temple in order to gain her protection and support. Anahita's blessing would bring fertility and abundance to the country.[4]

Time passes... history takes place... The Achaemenian empires falls to 'Alexander the Accursed'...

Circa 200 BCE sees the dedication of a Seleucid temple in western Iran to "*Anahita, as the Immaculate Virgin Mother of the Lord Mithra*".[5] The blend of Greek and Persian cultures manifest themselves in the Seleucid dynasty.

Time passes... history takes place...

The Parthian Empire (circa 247 BCE-226 CE) replaces the Seleucid and the Parthians expand the Anahita temple at Kangavar.

Time passes... history takes place...

Mark Anthony marches in to Armenia (circa 37 BCE - 34 BCE), and in one of the latter campaigns reached the Anahita temple at Erez:

> *"The temple of Erez was the wealthiest and the noblest in Armenia, according to Plutarch. During the expedition of Mark Antony in Armenia, the statue was broken to pieces by the Roman soldiers. Pliny the Elder gives us the following story about it: The Emperor Augustus, being invited to dinner by one of his generals, asked him if it were true that the wreckers of Anahit's statue had been punished by the wrathful goddess. 'No,*

---

4 Official entry on Anahita by the Embassy of the Islamic Republic of Iran in Ottawa, Canada on their Web site:
http://www.salamiran.org/Women/General/Women_And_Mythical_Deities.html
5 First Iranian Goddess of productivity and values by Manouchehr Saadat Noury - Persian Journal, Jul 21, 2005.
http://www.iranian.ws/iran_news/publish/printer_8378.shtml

answered the general, on the contrary, I have today the good fortune of treating you with one part of the hip of that gold statue.' The Armenians erected a new golden statue of Anahit in Erez, which was worshiped before the time of St. Gregory Illuminator."[6]

Time passes... history takes place...

The Sassanian Empire is formed ca. 226 CE. The Temple of Anahita in Bishapur was built during the Sassanian era (241-635 CE). The temple is believed to have been built by some of the estimated seventy thousand Roman soldiers and engineers who were captured by the Persian King Shapur (241-272 CE), who also captured three Roman emperors: Gordian III, Phillip, and Valerian. The design of the temple is noteworthy: water from the river Shapur is channelled into an underground canal to the temple and flows under and all around the temple, giving the impression of an island. The fire altar would have been in the middle of the temple, with the water flowing underground all around it. One might interpret this as a union of water—Anahita— with fire—Mithra.[7]

BRONZE HEAD OF THE GODDESS ANAHITA, HELLENISTIC GREEK, 1ST CENTURY BCE FOUND AT THE ANCIENT CITY OF SATALA, MODERN SADAK, NORTH-EASTERN TURKEY, NOW IN THE BRITISH MUSEUM.

6 A History of Armenia By Vahan M. Kurkjian, Bakuran. IndoEuropeanPublishing.com, 2008.
7 For the Temple of Anahita at Bishapur, see:

http://www.vohuman.org/SlideShow/Anahita%20Bishapur/AnahitaBishapur00.htm

The Temple of Anahita in Bishapur, Iran, on the site of the ancient city built by Shapur I, Sassanian Emperor (241 C.E.–272 CE) in celebration of his victory over three Roman Emperors - Gordian III, Phillip, and Valerian. (Photograph by Jamshid Varza, www.vohuman.org, reproduced here with his kind permission.)

25 | From a Drop of Water

Time passes... history takes place...

The Sassanian Empires fades and Islam arrives in Iran.

900 CE. Moslem pilgrims make their way to the 1100 year-old shrine of Bibi Shahr Banoo, the Islamic female saint, near the old town of Rey (South of Tehran). The town of Rey is thought to be 5000 years old, and the site of this shrine with its waterfall is believed by some to have once been an Anahita shrine. It is also close to the Cheshmeh Ali Hill (the spring of Ali Hill), which is dated to 5000 years ago. Perhaps this is an echo of Mithra-Anahita shrines being located close to each other and then becoming linked to later Islamic saints, a process seen frequently in Christianized Europe too; for example, sites sacred to the Celtic goddess Brighid became sites dedicated to Saint Brigit.

Furthermore, according to Susan Gaviri: *Anahita in Iranian Mythology* (1993):
> "...it must not be forgotten that many of the famous fire temples in Iran were, in the beginning, Anahita temples. Examples of these fire temples are seen in some parts of Iran, especially in Yazad, where we find that after the Muslim victory these were converted to Mosques."[8]

Time passes... history takes place...

Pilgrims continue to visit the Pre-Islamic Zoroastrian shrine of Pir e Sabz, or Chek Chek (*"drip drip,"* the sound of water dripping), in the mountains of Yazd. This is still a functional temple and the holiest site for present-day Zoroastrians living in Iran, who take their annual pilgrimage to Pir e Sabz Banu, *'the old woman in the mountain,'* also called Pir e Sabz, *'the green saint,'* at the beginning of summer. *Pir* means *'elder,'* and it can also mean *'fire.'* The title of Pir also connotes a Sufi master. *Sabz* means *'green.'*[9]

Pilgrims also continue to visit Pir e Banoo Pars (*'Elder Lady of Persia'*) and Pir e Naraki located near Yazd. The Pir Banoo temple is in

---

[8] Anahita in Iranian Mythology, p.7 (1993). This book is in Persian—translation here by Nabarz.
[9] For the temple at Pir-e-Sabz, see http://www.vohuman.org/SlideShow/Pir-e-Sabz/Pir-e-Sabz-1.htm

an area that has a number of valleys; the name of the place is Hapt Ador, which means Seven Fires.[10]

Time passes... history takes place...

COMMEMORATIVE GOLD COIN WITH IMAGE OF ANAHITA, 1997.

The Central Bank of Armenia in 1997, issues a commemorative gold coin with an image of Anahita on it. The bank states:

> "This commemorative coin issued by the Central Bank of Armenia is devoted to Goddess Anahit. Anahit has been considered the Mother Goddess of Armenians, the sacred embodiment and patron for the crop, fruitfulness and fertility. In 34 BC, the Romans have plundered the country town Yeriza of the Yekeghiats Province in the Higher Hayk, where the huge golden statue to Anahit was situated. They smashed the statue to pieces and shared among the soldiers as pillage. On the turn of the 19th century, a head part of a bronze statue referring to Anahit was found in Satagh (Yerznka region), which is presently kept in British Museum."[11]

Time passes... history takes place...

The higher social status of women in Iranian society compared to its Arab neighbours has been suggested by some to be due to its long respect for Lady Anahita. Indeed, the first Muslim woman to win a Noble Peace Prize (2003) was from Iran.

---

10 For the temples of Pir e Banoo Pars and Pir e Naraki, see http://www.sacredsites.com/middle_east/iran/zoroastrian.htm

Time passes.... history take place..... Yet she is still remembered....

"*Tomorrow (21.8.03), I (Jalil Nozari) will take part in a ceremony to commemorate a very poor, old woman, a relative of mine, who died recently. Her name was Kaneez. The name in modern Farsi has negative connotations, meaning a 'female servant.' But, in Pahlavi, the language spoken in central Iran before the coming of Islam, it meant 'a maiden,' a virgin, unmarried girl. Indeed, it has both meanings of the English 'maid.' Anahita, too, means virgin, literally not defiled. But this is not the end of story. When I was a child, there was a place in Ramhormoz, my hometown, which now is under a city road. In it, there was a small, single-room building with a small drain pipe hanging from it. Women in their ninth month and close to delivery time stood under this pipe and someone poured water through it. There was the belief that getting wet under the drain would assure a safe delivery of the baby. The building was devoted to Khezer (the green one). * Yet, the cult is very old and clearly one of Anahita's. The role of water and safe child delivery are both parts of the Anahita cult. My deceased aunt, our Kaneez, was a servant of this building. The building was demolished years ago to build a road, and Kaneez is no more. I wonder how will we reconstruct those eras, so close to us in time yet so far from our present conditions. It is also of interest that there exist remains of a castle, or better to say a fort, in Ramhormoz, that is called 'Mother and Daughter.' It belongs to the Sasanides era. 'Daughter,' signifying virginity, directs the mind toward Anahita. There are other shrines named after sacred women, mostly located beside springs of water. These all make the grounds for believing that Ramhormoz was one of the oldest places for Anahita worshippers.*"[12]

(* There is a folk tradition about Saint Khezer or Khidar (the green one): if one washes (pours water) on one's front door at dawn for forty days, he will appear. Khider is described as being a friend of the Sufis, and is said to stand at the boundary of sea and land. He is also said to have drunk from the fountain of immortality.)

---

11 http://www.cba.am/CBA_SITE/currency/aanahit.html?__locale=en
12 Personal communication from Jalil Nozari, August 20, 2003.

Time passes... 2004 CE.

GODDESS ANAHITA SCULPTURE BY JENNY RICHARDS (2009);
AMONG WATER LILIES, PHOTO BY P. NABARZ

Another seeker meditating by a sea makes an observation on relationships between Mehr and Aban (modern Persian names for Mithra and Anahita.) The Autumn Equinox marks the beginning of the Persian month of Mehr, and the start of the festival of Mehregan. The month of the sun god Mithra is followed by the month of the sea goddess Anahita (according to ancient sources both the partner and mother of Mithra). The month of the sun thus leads into the month of the sea. The sun sets into the ocean. The sunset over the ocean is one of the most beautiful sights there is; as the sun unites with the ocean, the light is reflected upon the water.

Mehr, coming together with Aban, gives rise to a third word: *mehraban*, which translates as *'kindness,'* or *'one who is kind.'* Thus, this metaphorical child of light that comes out of the marriage between Sun and Sea is *kindness*. The child of light is the Inner Light, which is in everyone. The Sun (light of God) and the Sea (divine ocean), united within each person, creates perhaps the most important spiritual quality - that of human kindness.

Time passes...

2777 C.E. Somewhere on a beach by the Caspian Sea. A young Magi has been keeping a night vigil. His solitary fire is the only light for miles around and his recitation of Aban Yasht, the hymn to angel-goddess Anahita, the only sound to be heard apart from the waves gently crashing onto the beach... She is remembered.

Further reading:
The Mysteries of Mithras: The Pagan Belief That Shaped the Christian World, by Payam Nabarz. Inner Traditions, 2005.
Wise Lord of the Sky: Persian Myth, by Tony Allan, Charles Phillips, and Michael Kerrigan. Myth and Mankind series. Time Life Books, 1999
Anahita in Iranian Mythology, (Anahita dar usturah ha-yi Irani), by Susan Gaviri. Tehran, Intisharat-i Jamal al Haqq, (year 1372), 1993.
First Iranian Goddess of productivity and values, by Manouchehr Saadat Noury in the *Persian Journal*, Iranian.ws, Jul 21, 2005.
The Avestan Hymn to Mithra trans. Ilya Gershevitch. Cambridge University Press, 2008.
The Heritage of Persia, by Richard N. Frye. Mazda, 1993.
Textual sources for the study of Zoroastrianism by Mary Boyce. University of Chicago Press, 1990.
Aban Yasht online translation at http://www.avesta.org/ka/yt5sbe.htm

DANCING WITH WATER

BY NINA FALAISE

Water has long been held sacred by ancient civilisations all over the world. Apart from the fact that water is life giving, it has the ability to reflect back to us our true nature, our soul.

Let us just touch upon what water has meant to some of the ancient cultures from around the world, before looking deeper into the sacredness of water and finally entering into the dance visualization, *'Dancing with Water'*.

In India the Ganges is considered to be one of the holiest of rivers. The river is believed to be the body of the Goddess Ganga, representing the feminine energy of the Universe that is connected to both life and death. According to Hindu belief, the Ganges purifies everything that it touches. Ritual cleansing with water is also an important aspect of the Shinto religion of Japan; one form of ritual cleansing is called *misogi*, and is performed to this day at the Tsubaki Grand Shrine, located at the foot of Mt. Hikiyama in Mei Prefecture. Here, by standing under a waterfall, the individual's *tama* (soul) becomes pure.

The ancient Mesopotamian people regarded the abyss of water as a symbol of the unfathomable, absolute Wisdom. In the *Vedas*, water is referred to as *'most maternal'*. In the *Koran* it cites that "We have created every living thing from water", and to the ancient Egyptians water was the primeval matter from which all creation began.

Hindu legend has it, according to the *Shiva Purana*, that when Lord Shiva opened his eyes after thousands of years of meditation, he saw the suffering of the earth's beings and tears came to his eyes out of compassion. A tear fell to earth becoming a seed, which grew into the sacred Rudraksha tree. Rudra is the name of Lord Shiva and Aksha means *'tear'*.

Scientifically speaking, according to Superstring Theory, the entire universe vibrates. Everything has its own unique vibration, from a lemon to an animal, a tree to a person, a thought to a word; every one of these has its own vibrational sound. Water is so sensitive to frequencies that it faithfully mirrors all the vibrations created in its surroundings and the world. Thus, if a river is honoured as sacred, it becomes sacred through all the positive thoughts, words and chants it absorbs from its surroundings. Likewise, we, who are made up of between 55% and 70% water, are affected by not only our surroundings, but also by every thought we think and every word we speak. One may consider the physical act of intercourse and love making, which depends on the fluids of the body to reach orgasm. Think of how the power of thought and feelings create the sensations leading to orgasm and the orgasm itself! Water is movement, and even when it appears still (as in a pond or lake) it is moving, continuously vibrating to the sounds of the universe.

So with these thoughts, let's move into *'Dancing with Water'* through the art of visualisation. Though this dance may seem to be for women only, it is also for men who wish to make contact with the feminine within themselves. It may be helpful to record the visualisation so that, without having to read, you can be ready to begin to dance when you feel moved to do so. Also, after each paragraph, give yourself time to visualise the scene you have just read. The spaces between the paragraphs indicate were you may spend time to visualise the scene. Pauses may be left silent in recording for as long as you feel you may need to bring the scene alive in your mind's eye. Once you have listened to the visualisation a few times, you will be able to leave it behind completely and just dance!

Find a space where you know you will not be interrupted for at least half an hour. Along with the recorded visualisation, you may like to choose some gentle background music to put on. The music could have harp or piano instruments in it, or anything that sounds like water.

Sit comfortably on the floor, but if the floor is not comfortable for you, then you may wish to sit on a chair. Close your eyes, breathe rhythmically and deeply, listening to your heart beat and looking within your own body. A significant fraction of the human body is water. Lean muscle tissue contains about 75% water by weight. Blood contains 95% water, body fat contains 14% water and bone has 22% water. Skin also contains much water.

With this information and awareness, imagine you can see, in your mind's eye, the waters of your body flowing through the blood, muscles, bones, body fat and skin. The inside of you body is like a landscape, and the waters like rivers making their journey through this landscape. See the rivers falling over bones and cascading like waterfalls, moving around glistening wet organs, running into crevices and along dark underground tunnels. See the rivers join together creating one big river rolling on to its next destiny.

Follow the river as it comes to an opening: it gushes out of the opening into the cave of a womb. The waters enter the cave to form a big lake. It is dark here, yet there is an opening on the ceiling of the cave, through which falls, like a thin veil, the silvery rays of the moon. Looking back at the lake, you see what seems to be a vortex appearing in its depths. There is a great whooshing sound, as the water turns ever faster, swirling around; you watch the fast movement of these dark waters. Sprays of water sprinkle onto your face: it is healing and cleansing. Out of the swirling waters, you see a strange ethereal being swimming so fast in the currents that it takes your breath away. Then, as if the waters follow her pace, she slows down to a halt, rising up like Venus at her birth from the sea-foam, and the waters become still and silent.

This nymph-like creature hovers, looking at her reflection in the waters of the lake. She has long wavy hair and big green eyes. A blue lotus frames the side of her delicate, almost fish-like face. As she lifts her head up, you see her eyes stare wildly into the distance. She sings a haunting song, which echoes, bouncing off the walls of the cave, sending rippling vibrations through the damp air.

Suddenly, she dives into the waters, with a big splash and whip of her fish-like body. At the same time, for a fraction of a moment, you feel like your head has gone under water. Just as suddenly YOU rise from the waters, out into a vast, open space, the sea. You are she and she is you, and you dance her dance of water.

Looking around at the vastness of the sea, you become aware that you can swim under and over the water with great ease. Your body is boneless, you are able to move with great curves, twists and turns. You are slippery as an eel. You are at one with the water, dancing, flowing, turning, diving down and lifting up to return to the surface.

You see a pod of dolphins in the distance swimming towards you and there is laughter in the sea-washed air. You join the dolphins, leaping and turning joyfully. Theirs is a language of rejoicing to the dance of life. You may be aware how they swim, with joy vibrating through every fibre of their being. You become aware of your own body. You explore every movement that your body can make; the turn of your head, the elegance of your arms, the gestures of your hands and fingers, the bends and twists of your waist and the supporting grace of your legs and feet. Your dance becomes ever more energetic as you swim, arching over the waves and diving into the folds of the waves. Under the water you hear the song of the dolphins. As you rise out of the water you hear the song of the albatross.

For a moment you stay still, floating on the surface of the waters, listening to the wisdom song of the albatross. All the sea becomes still waters with your stillness. As you look up to listen to the song, you see your reflection in the dark eye of the albatross. Then you look down and see your reflection through the shadow of the albatross crossing over the waters of the sea. You sink into your own reflection and dive deep down into the waters to find yourself back in the cave with the lake. Once again you are observing the inside of you body as a landscape.

The nymph dances, playfully creating ripples in the lake. You observe her graceful movements. As you watch, she leaps up into the damp air and spins round so fast, water splashes out from her wet body, in all directions. Her form changes becoming smaller and smaller until she is a drop of water falling into the lake and disappearing from sight.

You may listen to the beating heart of your inner world, sending pulsating waves throughout your body. Like the ebb and flow of the sea, the rhythmic beat draws you into yourself and out to your greater Self. Thus you express the very essence of your being throughout the Universe on the waves of sound initiated by one drop of water.

Bringing your awareness to your surroundings, ground yourself by becoming aware of the rhythm of your breathing and feeling the solidity of your body.

You may like to give a little thought of gratitude to the powers of water. Water is the nurturing life giver, without which we would not be. Yet without our collaboration with water, it can destroy the world and us. Great cities have been built and grow beside rivers and seashores. Great people are created through their collaboration and awareness of unseen processes within and around.

In the book *The True Power of Water* by Masaru Emoto, he says:
> "*We must pay respect to water, feel love and gratitude, and receive vibrations with a positive attitude. Then, water changes, you change, and I change, because both you and I are water.*"

THE MIRROR OF THE SOUL

ASSESSING THE FUNCTION OF WATERY RITUALS AND FOLK BELIEFS

BY YVONNE ABURROW

(DEDICATED TO PROF. RONALD HUTTON)

Water has always been important in ritual practice, and lakes, pools, bogs, rivers, wells and springs have all been objects of veneration, sites of ritual activity, or have acquired legends and folklore. So how did this symbolism develop, and why is water still an important symbol for us today?

In the late Bronze Age and early Iron Age, from around 1500 BCE to 100 BCE, it was customary to ritually deposit swords, pins, jewellery and other metal items in water. This occurred all over Europe; the Rhine was full of ritually deposited metalwork (Bradley, 1995:4); a hoard of bronze shields was found in Fröslunda, Sweden; various deposits have been found in the Thames, including the Battersea Shield, which is in the La Tène style (an early Iron Age style found all over Europe). Swords and daggers, bracelets and other jewellery have been found in rivers and bogs all over Europe. Even today, we still throw coins into fountains. A sword was deposited in a river as late as the fourteenth century. So why the urge to deposit metal in water? Richard Bradley (1995:4) suggests a connection between rites of passage such as entry into manhood and death and the votive deposition of metalwork into water. Certainly the Battersea shield does not look as if it would have been much use in battle, as it is thin and easily pierced by a spear, so it must have been purpose-made for ritual deposition. We also know that many *'Celtic'* peoples regarded watery places as entrances to the Otherworld, perhaps because of the reflective qualities of water; the way it reflects the landscape and the sky makes it look as though it is a gateway to another world. It is clear that these deposits are ritual because there are too many of them to be accidental losses, and because often the objects have been ritually *'killed'* - broken or bent - before being deposited.

However we must also be cautious about regarding every bog or river deposit as having been ritually placed there (bog bodies being a case in point, but also hoards hidden in ground which subsequently became waterlogged). Levy (cited in Bradley, 1995:11) identified a way of distinguishing between ritual and other deposits. She posited that ritual deposits all seemed to include objects of *'cosmic'* significance such as musical instruments and swords, and they also included food items and were located in water or in sacred places such as burial mounds. Other deposits were in dry ground, were buried less deep in the ground, and included a lot of tools and no food items - implying that they were placed there by someone hiding valuable items in times of stress.

Many legends describe the deposition of metalwork in water. For instance the *Nibelungenlied* has Hagen depositing gold in the river Rhine (though he plans to retrieve it later), and in Arthurian legend King Arthur receives the magic sword Caliburn or Excalibur from the Lady of the Lake, and it must be returned to her when he dies. It is also apparent from mythology that water was regarded as a gateway to the Otherworld. The legendary voyage to the Otherworld was over the western ocean. Kaiser (2003) suggests that the reason bogs and marshes were regarded as liminal places and entrances to the Otherworld was because of the marsh-lights, also referred to as corpse-candles:

> *"The appearance of the bog may be of interest. ... These waterlogged areas were certainly seen as sacred to the Celts, who made many ritual offerings in them. They may also be related to spirit travel, due to the appearance of marsh lights or 'corpse candles' in these waterlogged areas. Thought to be ignited marsh gas, these lights have variously been interpreted as fairies or spirits. Sometimes when corpse lights appeared they were said to be an omen of death and would trace the route of the impending funeral."*

The abode of the gods was sometimes seen as a magical island in the western ocean, or in the Summer Country, that is to say Somerset, which was waterlogged for much of the year before extensive drainage in the eighteenth and nineteenth centuries converted it into fertile farmland. That is perhaps how Glastonbury (Ynys Witrin, the Isle of Glass) got its name. Glastonbury Tor is also said to be the gateway to Annwn, the underworld, and the abode of Gwyn ap Nudd, the lord of that realm. Interestingly, Nudd or Nodens had a temple at Lydney on the other side of the River Severn, excavated by Mortimer Wheeler in the 1920s (and incidentally, one of his volunteer diggers was JRR Tolkien). Some of the chambers of this temple complex have been interpreted as dream incubation chambers (Trubshaw, 2008).

Many deities are associated with water, especially rivers. Usually river deities are goddesses, but Greek mythology has river gods too: Achelous and Meander. The goddess of the River Severn was called Hafren in Welsh, Sabrina in Latin. The river Tay in Perthshire, Scotland, was named after the goddess Tatha, whose name means *'the Silent One'* (and is pronounced as Tay). The river Ribble, which runs through North Yorkshire and Lancashire, is sacred to Belisama, a goddess connected with lakes and rivers, fire, crafts and light. The river Seine was sacred to the goddess Sequana, who was depicted riding in a boat with a duck-shaped prow. The River Dee was named for the goddess Deva; the River Wharfe, which means *'twisting'* or *'winding'*, for the goddess Verbeia; the River Wye for the goddess Vaga; The river Boyne in Ireland for the goddess Boann. According to the metrical *Dindshenchas* (Gwynn, 2009), Boann created the River Boyne by challenging the power of the well of Segais (where the salmon of wisdom ate the nuts of knowledge). She walked widdershins around the well, and this caused it to overflow and run down to the sea, and so the River Boyne was created, and she drowned in the flood. The goddess Brigantia gave her name to two rivers, the Brent and the Braint. The River Clyde was named after the goddess Clota. There are many other river goddesses around the world, the most famous being those of the Ganges and the Jumna rivers in India. A possible Gaulish river goddess (though not associated with a particular river) is Nantosuelta, whose name means *'winding river'*.

There are many holy wells and springs; they are too numerous to mention all of them. There is an excellent survey of the holy wells and springs of Bristol and Bath by Phil Quinn. Many sacred wells were said to cure ailments. Saint Keyne's well in Cornwall was resorted to by newly-married couples; whichever one of them drank from it first would gain the upper hand in the relationship. Some wells were associated with severed heads, one example being that of Saint Oswald, who was a

King of Northumbria. He was killed in a battle with Penda (the pagan King of Mercia) on 5th August 642 CE. There are two wells dedicated to him: one is at Winwick in Lancashire, the other at Oswestry in Shropshire. The Shropshire one is both a healing and a wishing well, and is used for divination. At the back of the well is a stone which used to be surmounted by a carved head wearing a crown; Saint Oswald's head is supposed to be buried there (Aburrow, 1993).

Another severed head legend pertains to Saint Winifred's Well in Wales; according to the *Welsh Fairy Book* (Thomas, 1908):

> "In the seventh century there lived a virgin of the name of Winifred, the daughter of noble parents: her father, Thewith, was a powerful noble, and her mother was sister to St. Beuno. After founding his monastery at Clynnog, St. Beuno visited his relatives in Flintshire, and, obtaining from his brother-in-law a piece of land, caused a church and convent to be erected on it; in charge of the convent he placed his niece Winifred. Caradoc, a neighbouring Prince, struck by her great beauty, tried to gain her in marriage, but, having dedicated herself to the service of God, Winifred would not listen to his suit. Thereupon the Prince attempted to carry her off by force, but she escaped from his hands and fled. Caradoc, enraged at his disappointment, pursued her, drew his sword and cut off her head. He instantly received the reward of his crime: he fell down dead, and the earth opening, swallowed his impious corpse. The severed head bounded down the hill and stopped near the church. Where it rested a great spring burst forth. St. Beuno, coming out of the church, where he had been preaching, took up the head and carried it to the corpse. After praying to God, he joined it to the body, and the virgin was restored to life, nor was there any sign of the wound to be seen other than a slender white line encircling her neck. Winifred lived fifteen years after this, and became the abbess of a convent at Gwytherin, in Denbighshire. The spring which burst forth on the spot where her head rested is still flowing, and its stones are annually spotted with blood in commemoration of the miracle. Ever since it has been believed to have virtues like those of the Pool of Bethesda, and great multitudes of sick folk, blind, halt and withered step into it to be made whole of their diseases."

It is difficult to tell what the motif of the oracular severed head with healing powers might have meant to ancient polytheists (though it could be that the head was regarded as the seat of the soul). Severed heads have been found in archaeological contexts in Gaul, though not in water. Diodorus Siculus recorded that Celtic warriors kept the severed heads of their slain enemies pickled in cedarwood oil (Mandrake Press, undated). The severed head of Bran the Blessed was kept in a magical house in Harlech and continued to speak. None of these heads are associated with water or wells, however. Perhaps the pagan Celtic obsession with severed heads was wedded to the Christian obsession with water to produce a new mythological theme. Christian symbolism is full of watery metaphors, because of the symbolism of baptism, but also the stream of water said to have flowed from Christ's side, and the *'living waters of the Spirit',* so the tradition of healing wells and springs is compatible with this symbolism, whether or not it predates Christianity.

One of the most famous sacred springs is that at Bath, where hot water gushes out of the earth, and is sacred to Sulis, the goddess of the waters. Her name has been variously interpreted as meaning *'eye'*, *'gap'* or *'sun'*. A hot spring was also associated with a goddess at Buxton (Aquae Arnemetiae, or the waters of the goddess of the grove). Hot springs are also regarded as sacred by indigenous Americans and the Japanese.

Various lesser spirits are also associated with water. The kelpie or water horse is a legendary Scottish beast that lures unwary travellers into rivers and streams, and can shapeshift. Water spirits are often regarded as treacherous because of the dual nature of water as a life-giving substance but also as a taker of lives by drowning (Parkinson, undated). The MacGregor family was said to possess a kelpie's bridle. In England there was a water spirit called the Neck (known in Germany as the Nixe). These spirits could shapeshift, and sometimes appeared as dragons, and liked to drag people into the water. Similarly, the Grindylow (made famous by its appearance in the Harry Potter books) was a Yorkshire water spirit that would grab little children with their long arms and fingers and devour them if they came close to the edge of pools, marshes, or ponds. Water is likely to have been seen as an abode of spirits or the entrance to the world of Faerie because of its mysterious qualities - sometimes it reflects the world above, and sometimes you can see into its depths; and it flows and changes.

Flood myths are also significant. The story of the flood that covers the whole earth is found in various mythologies. It has been suggested that this was because people found fossil shells in the mountains and thought that they had been deposited there by an ancient flood. The symbolism of the flood is the utter destruction of all that went before, and the inception of a new order of things.

But what does it all mean?

In assessing folk beliefs it is important not to regard them as *'fossils'* of earlier belief systems. This view comes from the evolutionary theory of folklore, which suggested that culture evolves towards rationalism, leaving pockets or fossils of irrational belief or custom behind in *'backward'* areas. In fact we know from observation that culture is far more fluid, perhaps even cyclical. An intellectual fashion catches on, then a reaction sets in, and then a reaction to the reaction. Ideas spread and change, permeating popular discourse, and rituals and customs are adopted and adapted over time to new social conditions. Very few rituals remain unchanged for centuries (the only example of unchanging ritual that I can think of is Eastern Christian Orthodox liturgy); even if the form remains constant, the meanings change according to context. A far more useful way of looking at folklore is its form and function: how it reinforces or transforms social structures, and how it fits into the context of other traditions (Trubshaw 2002).

So what would be the social function of depositing metalwork in water, or of well-dressing? Perhaps the ritual deposition of metalwork reminded the audience of the magical or divine origins of smithcraft, or reminded them that all good things came from the gods (thus reinforcing the power of those who claimed to speak for the gods), or functioned as a rite of passage, as Richard Bradley (1995:4) suggested. It's hard to know why people still throw coins into water. Maybe it is simply the alluring way that the metal shimmers underwater. Activities such as well-dressing brought the community together for a festival celebrating the importance of water, and wells and springs and their continuing purity would have been incredibly important in the days before piped water. Customs such as going to wells for cures perhaps also make sense in this context of the importance of pure water, and the healing minerals present in hot springs would also be useful as cures.

The symbolism of water also reflects its form and function. The sea often symbolises the unconscious mind (sometimes calm, sometimes turbulent, and usually deep and mysterious). Rivers can represent the journey of life, with birth at the spring in the mountains, and death as dissolution in the great sea of mind. Because water is used for washing, it is used to create ritual purity in most religions. Because it is used for drinking, it symbolises refreshment of the spirit. Because it changes shape to fit whatever vessel contains it, it represents fluidity and flexibility. It also represents emotion, another changeable and fluid quality.

Bibliography

The Sacred Grove: the mysteries of the forest by Yvonne Aburrow. Chieveley: Capall Bann Publishing, 1993
The Passage of Arms: an archaeological analysis of prehistoric hoards and votive deposits by Richard Bradley. Cambridge: CUP Archive, 1990.
The Metrical Dindshenchas ed. Edward Gwynn, [online.] Available from http://www.ucc.ie/celt/published/T106500C/text002.html (accessed 26.7.2009).
The Corpse Watcher: an Irish folktale may contain intimations of a native shamanic tradition by David Kaiser. In *Northern Earth 96*, pp 12-15 [online] Available from http://www.northernearth.co.uk/cwatch.htm (accessed 26.7.2009).
Celt, by Mandrake Press (undated), [online] Available from http://www.mandrake-press.co.uk/Definitions/celtic.html (accessed 26.7.2009).
Kelpie, by Daniel Parkinson (undated), *Mysterious Britain and Ireland*. [online] Available from http://www.mysteriousbritain.co.uk/scotland/folklore/kelpie.html (accessed 26.7.2009).
Holy wells of Bath and Bristol region, by Phil Quinn. Woonton Almeley: Logaston, 1999
The Welsh Fairy Book by W. Jenkyn Thomas (1908), [online] Available from http://www.sacred-texts.com/neu/celt/wfb/wfb63.htm (accessed 26.7.2009)
Explore Folklore by Bob Trubshaw. Market Harborough: Heart of Albion Press, 2002.
Dream incubation by Bob Trubshaw (2008), At the edge. [online] Available from http://www.indigogroup.co.uk/edge/dreaminc.htm (accessed 28.7.2009)

Special thanks to Mark Williams for help with the origins of severed heads in Celtic mythology. Any remaining errors are my own.

Married to the Sea

Eroticism in Ocean Lore

By Chrissy Derbyshire

When the world was young, when Time himself was just a dark little boy born of the Sky, the Goddess of Love rose up out of the sea. The great Sky God Uranus had angered Gaia, who urged her son to castrate the proud god as he slept. With a sickle young Cronos swiped, and the Sky God's genitals fell into the sea. When they hit the water it began to churn and foam. But from this act of violence, beauty was born. Out of the foam, riding upon a shell, rose glorious Aphrodite. Her long hair flowed like a wave in the sea breeze, and rivulets of water flecked with foam trailed down her naked body. Immortalised in art and literature, this otherworldly figure would go on to embody beauty, love and sexuality in the collective imagination for centuries afterward. Somehow we know in our blood that eroticism and the sea are inextricably linked. Sea lore is rich in sexual themes and imagery. Sirens sit on rocks in the midday sun, ready to drive any passing man mad with their irresistible song. Selkies, seal-women, play naked in the surf and may be taken by mortal men if their sealskins are hidden. Mariners sing filthy sea songs, hymns to whores and sodomy, while the goddesses and redoubtable women fronting their ships look tactfully away. Even today, erotica often looks to the sea and sea-lore for inspiration. Bright and dark, bawdy or sinister, the sexualisation of the sea in the human imagination is undeniable.

The sirens, the ultimate seductresses of the sea, were originally bird-women. It is unclear when or why they became mermaids. However, though their form has changed significantly, their behaviour has remained the same. The overriding mythological and popular function of the siren is to seduce. Lured by their ethereal song, men at sea would crash their ships into jagged rocks or jump into the water and drown in their eagerness to reach the source of the sound. The selkie of Scotch folklore is often mentioned in the same breath as the siren, though on the face of it their folkloric functions are very different.

The siren is a constant hybrid, always either half-bird or half-fish. The selkie takes a woman's form when naked but becomes a seal when she dons her sealskin. More importantly, while the siren is an inscrutable seductress, stories of selkies generally depict the creatures at innocent play. Indeed, in these stories it is frequently the mortal man who plays the seducer, stealing the sealskin so that the selkie forgets her true nature and persuading her to marry him. The greatest similarity between the two creatures is their contradictory nature, encompassing both desire and destruction. For want of the siren, men are drowned or dashed on rocks. For want of the selkie they father half-breed children who eventually follow their displaced and homesick mother back to the sea, never to be seen again. Both siren and selkie present a dangerous dual-mystery: the mystery of woman, and the mystery of the sea in one, strange and untameable.

There is an underlying darkness in the eroticism of ocean-lore that extends beyond myths of doomed lust for feral women. Perhaps it is partly because the very mystery that attracts us to the sea also acknowledges its untold capacity for danger. Yet this cannot be the whole story. There are some aspects of maritime folk tradition that are so devoid of mystery they seem almost anathema to the myths that (believed or not) ran alongside them. The sea chantey or shanty is notoriously simple, somewhat coarse and designed for the entertainment and morale of men who had been a long hard time at sea. When shanties deal with sex, the results are often creatively smutty and disgusting. Titles like *'Four Old Whores'* and *'Frigging in the Rigging'* leave little to the imagination. Their lyrics are similarly frank. In *'Four Old Whores'*, the titular women sing the praises of their magnificently vast private parts:

> *'The third old whore from Baltimore said*
> *Mine's as big as the sea.*
> *The ships sail in, the ships sail out,*
> *And leave their rigging free.'*

> *'Frigging in the Rigging' is less imaginative in its dirtiness:*
> *'There's frigging in the rigging,*
> *Wanking in the planking,*
> *Tossing in the crossing,*
> *There's fuck all else to do.'*

However, 'The Good Ship Venus', a song with a deceptively pleasant title, outstrips them all in the scope and nastiness of its vulgarity. To give just a few choice examples:

> 'On the Good Ship Venus,
> By Christ you should have seen us.
> The figurehead was a whore in bed
> Sucking a dead man's penis.
>
> ...
>
> The Captain's daughter Charlotte
> Was born and bred a harlot.
> Her thighs at night were lily-white,
> By morning they were scarlet.
>
> ...
>
> The cabin boy was Kipper.
> By Christ, he was a nipper.
> He filled his arse with broken glass
> And circumcised the skipper.'

So much for the Goddess of Love. Her Roman name, Venus, is used here presumably because of the link with sexuality, as well as its potential for an apt rhyme.

Despite its use of Venus' name, it seems clear that this song and others like it take little or no inspiration from mythical sources. One does not have to look far to recognise the source of their colourful imagery. Despite the humour and hyperbole, these songs are informed by the reality of sexuality aboard ship in the Age of Sail. From the 16th to the mid-19th century, when shanties were used to co-ordinate the movements of groups of sailors hauling on lines, morale was often very low among naval crews. Many seamen were forced aboard ship by press gangs, and once conscripted in the navy were kept there until their ship was decommissioned. Shore leave was hardly ever given, due to the likelihood of desertion. Living conditions were poor and pay was patchy, and low when it came at all. As such, to insure themselves against mutiny (as well as against the much-feared and taboo issue of homosexuality), commissioned officers routinely allowed prostitutes on board naval vessels to serve the men. In art and much popular literature, these prostitutes were portrayed as fat, jolly, overdressed and frequently old and ugly women. In reality, a large proportion of ship's prostitutes were very young and undernourished. Naval seaman William Robinson, active in the Royal Navy from 1805 to 1811, described the prostitutes coming aboard his ship when it moored in Portsmouth:

> "*Of all the human race, these poor young creatures are the most pitiable; the ill-usage and degradation they are driven to submit to are indescribable... Old Charon [the boatman who carries the women out to the ships] often refuses to take some of them, observing to one that she is too old, to another that she is too ugly, and that he shall not be able to sell them.*"[13]

The above description illustrates the true nature of sexuality aboard ship during the Age of Sail. Occasionally seamen's wives would be allowed aboard, but the line between wife and prostitute was often forcibly blurred. The only real alternatives to using degraded and impoverished women were celibacy (rare, and not especially lauded) and homosexuality (then known only as *'sodomy'* or *'buggery'* and highly taboo).

The sea, then, is a dark place for the exploration of sexuality. Mariners recognised this, and their songs and superstitions reflected it. Yet the association of eroticism with the sea never went out of vogue – not that it was ever a matter of fashion. It has been (from the beginning, if we put any stock in origin myths such as that of Aphrodite) a simple matter of fact. There is a particular Inuit myth, rare among sea/sex myths in that it has a happy ending. It could be said to highlight an arguably healthier attitude to the cycles of life and death and the power of sexuality as an expression of love. The story of Skeleton Woman goes like this:

There was a young girl who had angered her father somehow, and in his anger he had thrown her from a cliff into the sea. There she sank, and over the years her flesh dissolved until she was nothing but stark bones and long, black hair. Then no fishermen would seek fish in that part of the sea, fearing it was haunted. One day, however, a fisherman who had not heard the rumours came and let his line out in that haunted patch of water. He felt a mighty pull on the line and excitedly reeled in what he thought must be a monster fish. He turned for a second to ready his nets, and when he turned back the terrifying Skeleton Woman had clawed her way blindly up the line and was

---

13 Robinson, William, Jack Nastyface: Memoirs of a Seaman. Naval Institute Press, 1973, quoted in Stark, Suzanne J. Female Tars: Women Aboard Ship in the Age of Sail. Pimlico, 1998.

staring at him with empty, waterlogged eye sockets. He began to row away, sorely frightened, but she appeared to follow him. In reality, she was just tangled in his line. When he reached the shore he gathered up his equipment and began to run, but she was still tangled up and continued to follow him. She followed him right into his house, where he collapsed in fear and soon noticed that she, too, had stopped advancing on him. Instead she was lying sprawled on the floor, all tangled bones and hooks and netting, and all at once his heart was filled with pity for her. So the fisherman set about untangling her, cleaning the seaweed and barnacles from her tired bones, and brushing her long hair. Then, exhausted, he fell asleep. Nobody knows what he dreamt that night, but the story goes that in his slumber he wept a single tear, which dropped into the dead mouth of Skeleton Woman. She drank of that single tear thirstily, and it brought her to life. Then, gently as a caress, she took out his heart as he slept and began to beat upon it like a drum. And with every beat she drummed wholeness into herself. She drummed for flesh and she drummed for skin, she drummed for strong muscles and soft curves, for eyes and lips and a tongue. Then, when she was complete, she replaced the heart back in the sleeping man's chest and lay down beside him. When they awoke they were tangled again, in each other, and neither ever wanted to move away.

Such is the mystery of sexuality and the sea. The sea can and frequently does bring death and destruction, yet it brims with life more varied and wonderful that even modern man can imagine. It is the great giver, the great taker, remaining inscrutable and mysterious whether approached with reverence, with longing or with unruly mirth.

Bibliography

Lao, Meri. *Seduction and the Secret Power of Women: The Lure of Sirens and Mermaids.* Park Street Press, 2007.
Pinkola Estés, Clarissa. *Women Who Run with the Wolves: Contacting the Power of the Wild Woman.* Rider, 1992.
Stark, Suzanne J. *Female Tars: Women Aboard Ship in the Age of Sail.* Pimlico, 1998.

Discography

Various Artists. *Rogue's Gallery: Pirate Ballads, Sea Songs and Chanteys.* Anti Records, 2006.

THE ADMIRAL, THE SIREN AND WHALE

WATER SPIRITS IN THE VODOU TRADITION

BY KIM HUGGENS

The Vodou tradition is as varied in praxis and belief as its adherents are in background, gender, age, and location. Historically speaking, the many strands of influence that united in the New World to create this syncretic religion testify to this manifold variety; the beliefs and spirits of African tribes from North, West, and South Africa mixed with the new Catholicism imposed upon the slaves brought over from those areas, the Native American ways of life they met in the Taino, Carib, and Arawak lands, the European folk magic and grimoire tradition brought over by indentured servants from the British Isles, and Freemasonic rites and symbolism. Thus, it is important to note at the beginning that the Vodou practices in different regions bear slightly different features – the practices of Northern Haiti are different to those of the South, and certainly very different to those found in New Orleans. However, similarities and shared features exist throughout, and Vodou also shares a number of similarities with other traditions that have come from the same root, such as Candomble and Santeria. One of the most important strands of symbolism found in most, if not all, Vodou traditions, is that of water and the spirits that relate to it. It may also be unsurprising that a tradition that in many cases developed on islands (such as Haiti) or coastal regions of the Americas, and which came into being through transportation halfway across the world on a ship, should hold within it such striking aquatic symbolism.

A note on terms

'Spirits' is one possible translation of the terms most often used to describe the beings that permeate the Vodou worldview. Terms such as lwa, loa, zange (from the French word for angel), les invisibles, saint, and mystére are also used interchangeably throughout the literature, and hint at the nature of the spirits (I will use the term lwa in this article.) Saints are usually associated with the lwa; but where some

SIX OF SWORDS (AGWE) FROM SOL INVICTUS: THE GOD TAROT
BY KIM HUGGENS AND NIC PHILLIPS. SCHIFFER BOOKS, LTD., 2007

Sources and traditions say they are the same, others say they are merely identified. The extent of this identification and the complex relationship between saint and lwa is discussed widely in the work of Melville J. Herskowitz.[14] One final point to make before beginning this discussion of the lwa associated with water, is that there are hundreds, if not thousand of lwa, a point made eloquently by Simpson:

"*All told there are hundreds of loas. One peasant said that the number of the loas is infinite, another said that while one cannot possibly know all of the loas it is important during a ceremony to invite all of them. Still another, a houngan's assistant, said that he is not concerned with knowing the names of all the loas, but insisted that in a ceremony he can easily summon all of them.*"[15]

Thus, what follows is only a very small fraction of the lwa, and those mentioned are only some of those I am aware of – some may appear in different forms in other houses and traditions.

Beneath the Waters and On the Underside of the Mirror

The lwa are often said to come from, and reside in, the '*land beneath the waters*' or Guinee (also called Ginen). In some traditions this watery realm is synonymous with the concept of ancestral Africa. However, it must be remembered that this '*Africa*' is not only the one from which the slaves were taken, but also scientifically speaking the home and origin of the bloodlines of every living human. Thus, the lwa are identified as having the same origin as all humans, which could in some way also be called God.

One ritual song for a spirit named Quitta (who is not a spirit associated with water) says:

Oh, Quitta oh so'ti nan dlo,   *Oh Quitta comes out of the water,*

li tout mouille!   *he is dripping wet!*

---

[14] Herskowitz, Melville J., African Gods and Catholic Saints in New World Negro Belief. American Anthropologist, New Series, vol. 39, no. 4, Part 1 (Oct-Dec 1937), pp. 635-643.
[15] Simpson, George Eaton, The Belief System of Haitian Vodun. American Anthropologist. New Series, vol. 47, no. 1. (Jan.-March 1945), pp.35-59.

Oh nen point houngan passe	There is no houngan who surpasses
Bondye nan pays-ya!	God in this country![16]

This indicates the lwa in question has come out of water in order for it to be present at the ceremony. Another song, this time for no spirit in particular but rather a ceremonial song announcing the intention of the mambo (priestess) to call upon the lwa, says:

Anonse o zanj nan dlo,	Alert the angels down in the water,
Bak odsu miwa.	Beneath the mirror.
O, l'a we, l'a we.	Oh, he will see, he will see.
Nou pral nan Vil-o-Kan ye.	We're going to Ville-aux-Camps.
Kreyol mande chanjmen, vre.	Creoles ask for change, truly.[17]

The author who recorded this song, Kathy Brown, commented that:
> "The spirits live on the back side of the mirror surface of the water. [...] In Vodou, the mirror is the principle accoutrement of Agwe, the male sea spirit, [...] The connection of mirrors, water, and Ginen, the home of the spirits, makes a complex, uroboric point. Gazing into the water, a woman sees her own reflection, and through it, simultaneously, she sees the lwa. Superimposed on the faces of the lwa she sees the faces of her ancestors, because an ancestor returns to the living in the form of a lwa he or she revered most during life."[18]

Not only the lwa but also the dead are said to live beneath these same waters, and so they can be viewed as the ancestral waters – a symbolic representation of the waters of the womb and the waters from which primordial creatures first emerged.[19] However, these Ginen waters are not such that when a soul enters them after death they

---

16 Courlander, Harold, Gods of the Haitian Mountains. The Journal of Negro History, vol. 29, no. 3, (July 1944), pp. 343.
17 Brown, Kathy. Mama Lola: Vodou Priestess in Brooklyn, pp. 284.
18 Brown, Kathy. Mama Lola: Vodou Priestess in Brooklyn, pp. 284.
19 Though there are many varied views on the soul's destination after death, many of them discussed in Simpson, The Belief System of Haitian Vodun, pp. 52-3.

would be able to recognize the souls of their relatives in life. One song says:

Dlo kwala manyan,	Water kwala manyan [langaj[20]]
Nan peyi sa maman pa konn petit li,	In that country the mother does not know her child,
Nan peyi sa fre pa konn se lie,	In that country the brother does not know his sister,
Dlo kwala manyan.	Water kwala manyan [langaj].

It is possible in Vodou to recall the spirits of one's ancestors from these waters however; certain death rites are used directly after death as well as after a certain time period after death to help separate the soul from its lwa and give it freedom. In some traditions, these souls are called up and housed in pots called govis, so that they may reside in the hounfor (temple) and continue to converse with and work with the living members of that family and community.[21] It is also said that Baron Samedi and Maman Brigitte, the mother and father of the cemetery and leaders of the Ghede and the dead, sometimes pluck a soul from the depths of these waters to become a lwa. The reasons for this process are unknown, and seemingly random, though it is believed that in some cases souls who were powerful houngans or mambos, or great people, in life, are more likely to become lwa.

Some modern commentators might suggest that in a psychological model of magick the origin of the lwa from *'the land beneath the waves'* suggests they come from our unconscious/subconscious minds. This may be supported by the fact that whilst it is said all lwa come from beneath the water, many are said to also live elsewhere and have a physical home, e.g. waterfalls, certain trees, or rocks. Thus, it could be suggested that the lwa that lives in trees (such as Neg Za Zi or Gran Bwa) also comes from the waters (our subconscious). Whether this psychological view is correct or not is a point not to be discussed here;

---

20 Langaj means "language", and refers in the context of Vodou songs and ceremonies to words that are not Creole or any language recognisable. Some believe that it is the language of old Africa, or a sacred language direct from Ginen, and in this sense it may be viewed in a similar manner to the Enochian of Dee and Kelly, or the phenomenon of speaking in tongues.
21 See Maya Deren's account of this ritual in Divine Horsemen: The Living Gods of Haiti, pp. 46-53.

however, I have seen this view as well as others held by several practitioners who are equally efficacious and successful with the work.

Although all lwa are said to come from the waters, certain lwa have a stronger connection to the physical waters of our everyday lives: oceans, rainstorms, springs, waterfalls, rivers, lakes, and tears.

Met Agwe Tawoyo

The Admiral of the Seven Seas, Met Agwe Tawoyo, is usually seen as a mulatto (coffee-cream coloured skin) man of noble bearing, wearing the uniform of a Navy Admiral, with green-blue eyes. Sometimes he is depicted with a fishtail, particularly when shown alongside his wife, Mambo La Sirene, who is a mermaid. Agwe's ship is called Imammou, and it is this vessel that carries the souls of the dead under the sea and to the land beneath the waves described above. This symbolism, so obviously reminiscent of the slaves being carried to the New World in slavers ships, sets Agwe up in the Western mind as a psychopomp and guide of souls, second only to Baron Samedi and his graveyard entourage in the task of eternal ferryman of souls.

Courlander has suggested that Agwe originated in the Yoruba lands of West Africa,[22] and was carried with the slaves across the water. His temperament can vary from melancholic (being reminiscent of a drowned sailor, in my experience), to noble and aristocratic, to furious. As Tawoyo his temper brings about thunderstorms and lightning over the ocean, the kind of storms that ships' crews fear the most, and it is said that the sounds of thunder are Agwe Tawoyo's cannons firing from his ship across the water. Sometimes in possession the *'horse'* being *'ridden'* by Agwe (the person being possessed by him) will climb onto a chair and use a pole to *'row'* the *'boat'*, sometimes causing the chair to sway wildly from side-to-side as if tossed on stormy waters. However, he is also beloved by many devotees, particularly those who may be attracted to the strong silent type:

> *"I think that in the heart of most mambos, and of most women servitors, Agwe holds a special place... it is Agwe who is, in a sense, the ideal husband and lover, being, as the sea is, both immediate and enduring, both a ready strength and a deep peace."*[23]

---

[22] Courlander, Gods of the Haitian Mountains. . The Journal of Negro History, vol. 29, no. 3, (July 1944), pp. 353.
[23] Deren, Maya, Divine Horsemen: The Living Gods of Haiti, pp. 125.

Still, there remains a melancholy about Met Agwe, a sadness that is not overwhelming but ever-present. Maya Deren describes the possession of two devotees by Agwe during a ceremony for him on a boat:

> *"...Agwe spoke a few words of greeting in a voice which gurgled as if with rising air bubbles, and seemed truly to come from the waters. His mood was not displeased, but it was sober. The houngan, conscience-stricken, began to explain that he, too, would soon make a ceremony. The two Agwes listened to him, their eyes at once forgiving and somehow detached. One thought: perhaps they forgive because they are detached. And, with the same air of noble, gentle sadness, the looked slowly from person to person, from the barque of food, to the mambo. There was something in their regard which stilled everyone. One had seen it in the faces of those who prepare to leave and wish to remember that to which they will no longer return."*[24]

This strong sadness comes across as a yearning for something out of reach that is not the romantic yearning of young lovers, but instead the awareness of something once had but now lost, an ever-present awareness of the distance between; the distance between a life across the waves in old ancestral Africa and that lived in the New World.

As Admiral of the Seven Seas, Agwe is surpassingly rich, with all the treasures of the ocean at his command. Long-lost sunken treasure ships are in his domain, the life that teems in colour and in darkness is the tapestry on his walls; prayers to Agwe for wealth and fortune are often answered. His authority also gives Agwe an impressive entourage of other lwa who form part of his crew on Imammou or follow the ship throughout the ocean. These include La Sirene, Ogou Balendjo, Ogou Yamsan, Silibo, Agasou Jemen, Erzulie Freda (although she also has her own entourage), La Baleine, Klemezine Klemey and President Klemeille (the latter two sometimes said to be Agwe's sister and father respectively.[25]) Nearly all of Agwe's entourage are associated with water, with cleansing, healing, removing negativity, and purifying. Met Agwe is also known for his several wives and mistresses – although an Admiral, it is clear he has the habits of a sailor when he makes berth! Among his

---

[24] Deren, Maya, Divine Horsemen: The Living Gods of Haiti, pp. 125.
[25] Fleurent, Gerdés. Dancing Spirits: Rhythms and rituals of Haitian Vodou, the Rada Rite, pp. 89.

lovers are the mermaid La Sirene, the luxurious Erzulie Freda, the ever-youthful Silibo, and the rainbow herself Aida Wedo, also the wife of the father serpent Damballah Wedo. One song sung for Agwe calls on him to be reasonable in his dealing with the ensnared hearts of these spirits (and, presumably, of the humans who are likewise infatuated with him):

Agwe-o-Agwe	*Agwe, O Agwe*
Ou pake kondui de fanm	*You can't lead two women*
Voye youn ale-o	*Send one of them away*
Se lan lanmé	*It's in the sea*
Se la Agwe rete	*It's where Agwe lives*
Agwe-o-Agwe	*Agwe, O Agwe*
Ou pake kondui de fanm	*You can't lead two women*
Voye youn ale-o	*Send one of them away.*[26]

Unsurprisingly in an environment where seafaring, trading, and fishing is often important, Agwe is called upon in coastal regions to protect anybody travelling over the sea or working upon it. He is the spirit that can see sailors safely through a storm, and symbolically sees his devotees through the rough storms of their lives. A beautiful song for him, recorded by William Seabrook during his research in Haiti says:

Agwe, woyo woyo!	*Agwe, woyo woyo!*[27]
Mait' Agwe reter lans la mer,	*Master Agwe lives in the sea,*
Li tirer canot.	*He is the lord of ships.*
Bassin blé	*In a blue gulf*
Reter toi zilet;	*There are three little islands;*
Neg coqui' lans mer zorage;	*The negro's boat is storm tossed;*
Li tirer cano la.	*Father Agwe brings it safely in.*
Agwe, woyo woyo!	*Agwe, woyo woyo!*[28]

---

26 Fleurent, Gerdés. Dancing Spirits: Rhythms and rituals of Haitian Vodou, the Rada Rite, pp. 90. Note that the Creole "kondui", here translated as "lead" more closely has connotations with the French "conduit", meaning "drive". Presumably the original song is earthier than the translator gives credit for.
27 This expresses feelings of surprise, excitement, or incredulity, in much the same way as the stereotypical Jew says "oi vey", or the young Southern belle might declare "oh my!"
28 Seabrook, William. The Magic Island, pp.58.

NURTURER (QUEEN) OF CUPS (LA SIRENE) FROM PISTIS SOPHIA: THE GODDESS TAROT BY KIM HUGGENS AND NIC PHILLIPS. DECK IN PROGRESS. © NIC PHILLIPS 2008

Mambo La Sirene

The seductive, inspiring, beautiful, and mysterious La Sirene is a lwa born from imagination and desire. As a mermaid she possesses all the associations of these mythical figures most commonly depicted singing and combing their hair on rocks by the sea.[29] Indeed, in possession La Sirene will usually be provided with a mirror and comb, or she will croon sweetly and wordlessly to herself and "swim" in the water (devotees will place a white sheet beneath her so she is not swimming on a dirty floor!) Those who work with her are usually gifted with artistic ability, poetry, a beautiful singing voice, and a vivid imagination. However, La Sirene can also be a dangerous spirit to work with, as she has the power to drown those she dislikes or likes too much. Thus, her devotees are careful never to submerge their heads underwater in a living body of water, so that they will not be possessed by La Sirene during their swim and drowned in her loving arms.

Some sources give La Sirene an origin in the more southern tribes of Africa, such as the Kongo,[30] whilst Herskowitz implies that La Sirene *"is a character derived from European mythology"*.[31] This is supported by Kathy Brown and expanded to further explain the character of this lwa:

> *"Some suggest that the persona... was derived from the carved figures on the bows of the ships of European traders and slavers. Thus the Vodou lwa Lasyrenn may have roots that connect, like nerves, to the deepest and most painful parts of the loss of homeland and the trauma of slavery. It is therefore fitting that she also reconnects people to Africa and its wisdom. In many stories, people are captured by Lasyrenn and pulled under the water, down to Ginen. Sometimes these stories are descriptions of tragic drownings or of suicides."*[32]

Indeed, some modern interpreters have seen in La Sirene the loving arms of the ocean accepting the slaves who jumped, still chained to

---

[29] For an excellent study of these associations, and thereby an acquaintance with La Sirene, read Lao, Meri. Seduction and the Power of Women: the Lure of Sirens and Mermaids. Vermont: Park Street Press, 1998.
[30] Filan, Kenaz. The Haitian Vodou Handbook: Protocols for Riding with the Lwa, pp. 103.
[31] African Gods and Catholic Saints in New World Negro Belief. American Anthropologist, New Series, vol. 39, no. 4, Part 1 (Oct-Dec 1937), pp. 639.
[32] Brown, Kathy. Mama Lola: Vodou Priestess in Brooklyn, pp. 223-4.

each other, into the waves to escape their fate in the New World. In a modern context, this voluntary jumping into the water can be seen as immersing ourselves in the imagination, fantasy, dreams, and visions. Some of the best healers, visionaries, and artists walk with La Sirene, and many of them describe the act of finding inspiration as swimming in an ocean of possibilities, surrounded by the fantastical creatures of their mind – such as mermaids.

For many devotees La Sirene also functions as a reflection, and the mirror she holds up to herself in her preening is also held up to us. This reflection is of our true selves, and therefore far more powerful than most people can imagine when they initially think of this – seemingly tame and harmless – mermaid.

> *"She is a fleeting presence, never fully seen, hinting at something monumental – huge, deep, sudden, and powerful. When people catch a glimpse of Lasyrenn beneath the water, they feel her beckoning them to come with her back to Ginen, to Africa, the ancestral home and the dwelling place of the lwa, anba dlo (beneath the water)... Gazing at her is like gazing at your own reflection. It is seductive because she gives a deeper and truer picture of the self than is likely to be found in the mirrors of everyday life."*[33]

This immense knowledge and wisdom, in my experience, is symbolised by the treasure beneath the waves that is given to La Sirene by her husband Agwe. La Sirene possesses the treasures of our innermost selves, our desires, our imagination; she is the X that marks the spot, and the map that shows the way; we follow her song to its source and then dig as deep as we can (into our subconscious, perhaps) to hopefully find gold. When we make wishes and toss coins into wells and springs, those wishes are carried down to the sea with the inevitability of rivers, and are taken to La Sirene – and some of them become the gold on the ocean when the sunlight hits the waves.

It is important to note that although La Sirene is similar to the Yoruban Yemanyá, the two are very distinct spirits and are closer to cousins or distant sisters. They are not the same spirit, and the offerings given to one may offend the other (for instance, La Sirene enjoys fish and oysters, whereas Yemaya is the mother of the fishes and to offer up her children as food to her would be unthinkable.) These spirits are different in a very important way: Yemaya is maternal, La Sirene is not. Though some sources suggest La Sirene had a child named Ursule whom she lost, this lwa is not appealed to for fertility and childcare. She is the playful waves and the beauty of sunlight on water surface rather than the fertile depths.

La Sirene is said to have a sibling – in some traditions a brother, in others a sister – called La Baleine (*'the whale'*). Whilst La Sirene is the sunlit surface of the waves, La Baleine is the dark, hulking, unfathomable depths of the ocean, into which no light can penetrate. This is not to say that La Baleine is malevolent at all, simply that he/she represents an all too human fear of the unknown – manifested here as the creatures of the sea that seem so alien to us, and in some cases very frightening: the whales looming out of the gloom; the strange skeletal fish in the deep sea; sharks hunting... In most Vodou traditions in order to work with La Baleine you must do so through La Sirene.

Damballah Wedo

Although in traditional Vodou cosmology the figure of God is held in highest esteem and given the most power, this figure is transcendent and in most cases almost completely removed from creation. Many Vodouisants will only refer to God in the male gender for ease in a climate that is predominantly Catholic. This transcendent being is usually viewed as creating the lwa to act as avatars or manifestations of God on earth and in the lives of humans. Out of all the lwa, Damballah Wedo, the great white python, is closest to God and therefore the purest.

Imagined as a serpent – usually white – Damballah is said to be married to Aida Wedo, the rainbow. Some traditions have these lwa as both serpents and rainbows, but the imagery here seems purely incidental – both the serpent and the rainbow have similar symbolic underpinnings. Both span across a distance and represent a connection between one thing and another. Specifically in the case of the serpent, the idea of *'As Above, So Below'* is represented by the upright snake with its head in heaven and its tail on the earth. In the Vodou tradition this upright snake is more obviously the *poteau mitan* – the pole in the centre of the *hounfor* that goes from the ceiling to the ground, up and down which the lwa and other spirits descend and

---

33 Brown, Kathy. Mama Lola: Vodou Priestess in Brooklyn, pp. 223.

ascend, making possession and other forms of communication with the spirit world possible. This spanning of a distance has reference to the drawing down of moisture in the form of rain as well, and thus Damballah is seen as a lwa who brings rainfall and pure springs:

> *"In Haiti, Aida Hwedo has become Ayida Wedo, the wife of Danbala. Together, the two (both are serpents and rainbows) arch over the broad ocean. Alternately, the rainbow and its reflection in the water below turn the serpent into a circle. Some say Danbalah has one foot- that is, the end of the rainbow – on the ocean where he draws up moisture, which he then deposits in the form of life-giving water through the other foot planted firmly in the mountains of Haiti. Danbalah thus moves between the opposites of land and water, as snakes do, uniting them in his coiling, uroboric movements, generating life. Danbala also tunnels through the earth, as snakes do, connecting the land above with the waters below."*[34]

The concept of the '*waters below'* has already been discussed as a place of origin for spirits and the dead, and thus the role of Damballah is essential to any Vodou ceremony.

Traditionally Damballah is the purest, cleanest lwa. He detests alcohol and smoking, and thus he is saluted towards the beginning of any ceremony, not only highlighting his importance to the Vodou universe but also ensuring nobody has had the chance to sully the ritual area with alcohol or smoke (that is often requested/consumed by other lwa.) It is perhaps logical to accept the symbolism of Damballah's fresh springs and rains as that of purity and cleanliness – the physical cleanliness facilitated by water also cleans the spirit, soul, and heart. In Haiti where clean water can sometimes be scarce and Vodouisants regularly come to ceremonies after a hard day's work, it is also highly valued. To bathe and clean oneself ready to serve the lwa is an act of dedication, respect, and recognition of the purity of some of the lwa.

The Simbis

Damballah is not the only snake to be found in Vodou mythology: the family of Simbis are all imagined as snakes of various kinds, and interestingly they are all water snakes. This either indicates a symbolic

---

34 Brown, Kathy. Mama Lola: Vodou Priestess in Brooklyn, pp. 274.

link in the Vodou system between snakes and water, or simply that most species of snake in Haiti can be found near water.

Simbi Dlo (Simbi *'of water'*, from the French *de l'eau*) is specifically associated with clean water that can be drunk, such as that of rain, springs, and taps. Altars and shrines to this lwa often consist of a well or spring in or around which small green snakes make their home.[35] Whereas Damballah's snake form is that of a pure white python, the snakes of the Simbis are usually smaller, thinner, and green. Simbi Andezo (Simbi *'in two waters'*, from the French *en deux eau*) is the lwa of water where saltwater and freshwater merges, such as the salt swamps of Haiti and America. Other Simbis, such as Simbi Makaya, Simbi Ganga, and Simbi Anpaka all live in water of some kind, and most are associated with magic, healing, and communication. In some sources they are the ones who – like Damballah – allow for the traversing of the distance between the worlds of both human and lwa souls:

> "It is the voodoo Mercury who conducts the soul from the visible to the invisibles, starting from the crossroads, and who then leads the invisibles to the crossroads, to receive the sacrifice. The voodoo Mercury has the name of Simbi, a loa of many forms. He is the conductor of souls, who leads the souls of the dead in all directions bordered by the four magical orients of the cross. He is the Messiah of Legba, the messenger of the sun. Simbi corresponds to the hermetic Mercury of the cabalistic alchemy of the ritual sacrifice... Simbi is the creative principle of the seminal vesicle because, in Voodoo tradition, Legba as the center post is himself the principle of the magic wand."[36]

It is a possibility that owing to the symbolism of snakes, as well as the nature of water to carry things and flow over distances, that the role of psychopomp has been applied to the Simbis as well as to Damballah. Certainly considering it was ships over the water that brought Vodou into being, and coupled with the role of Agwe as post-death psychopomp is his ship Imammou, it is tempting to draw a definitive link between the image of snake, water, boat, mirror and liminality.

---

35 Courlander, Gods of the Haitian Mountains. . The Journal of Negro History, vol. 29, no. 3, (July 1944), pp. 358.
36 Rigaud, Milo. The Secrets of Voodoo, pp. 93.

However, the Simbi are not always beneficent in their relations to humans, and like the lwa La Sirene above, they are credited with taking people underwater with them:

> *"The Simbi in general are aquatic vodouns, guardians of springs and ponds. They are well known for their abduction of light skinned (mulatto type) children while they are collecting water at a spring or river. The children are taken underwater, in the aquatic subterranean abode of the simbi vodouns where they work as servants. After some years, the simbi send them back to the surface of the earth with the gift of clairvoyance."*[37]

It is interesting to note that the Simbis and La Sirene all share the fact that they are lwa that live in places of water – unlike Agwe who sails over it, Damballah who brings it, and others who interact with water in some way but who have habitation elsewhere. Perhaps it is the fact that they are not beings of earth that they have such alien ideas and thought processes to our own? Perhaps by living in water they are wholly submerged in the fantastical realm it represents, and therefore are unbalanced in some way? Or perhaps, as liminal Mercurial figures, they invite us to move to a different experience of the world around us.

Agasou Jemen and Silibo Nouvavou

Part of Agwe's crew, Agasou Jemen is a sea warrior of Dahomean origin,[38] often called upon for his fierce vigour, ardour, and stoicism. He is a brave fighter, and can be imagined leading a sea battle or attack on land. He is also depicted in the form of a crab, and in possession his horse will crook and stiffen his hands like claws.[39] Although he is a spirit associated with the sea, it is Agasou's martial prowess that is elevated, in much the same way as Agwe is praised for his cannon-fire (thunder over the ocean) and is a spirit that would be a formidable opponent. Spirits such as these remind us – especially in the Western world – that water is not just symbolic of purity, nurture, and life, but also maintains a fiercely destructive form that brings devastation at certain times.

One song for Agasou, played fast and loud to martial drumming, extols these virtues:

---

37 Crosley, M.D., Reginald. The Vodou Quantum Leap, pp. 106.
38 Rigaud, Milo. The Secrets of Voodoo, pp. 141.
39 Rigaud, Milo. The Secrets of Voodoo, pp. 31.

Agasou Jemen   *Agasou Jemen*
Prete'm pistole ou-la   *Lend me your pistol*
Ou deja, gason lagé   *You're already a man of war*
Ou pap mouri san pale   *You won't die without talking.* [40]

This song is explained by its recorder, who brings to our attention this stoic nature of Agasou:

> *"The word jemen in Creole means 'to sprout' and refers to those of the same lineage, such as first cousins and brothers. Because of the close relationship, one feels safe enough to ask to borrow a pistol from one's brother. Agasou Jemen, in this context, means 'Agasou, my brother'. Agasou is a man of war, and as such, he will not die without speaking out. Furthermore, he is asked for his pistol, which means his vigour. One should recall that historically, to speak out (particularly in a political context) in Haiti could literally result in someone's death. But most Haitians will speak out in due time regardless of consequences. Therefore, this song is a song of challenge, a constant reminder of this aspect of the lwa, and, by extension, the Haitian psyche."* [41]

In many traditions Agasou is married to Silibo, sometimes called Silibo Nouvavou, a feminine lwa who is also found in Agwe's entourage and seems to have ancient origins and hint at something very primal. Milo Rigaud writes of her that she represents being *"initiated or loved by the sun... This is the voodoo lwa alone which unites the most magic forces... represents omniscience in voodoo."* [42] Anybody familiar with Kabbalistic symbolism at this point may be reminded of the role of Tiphereth on the Tree of Life, as the solar sephiroth that connects like a spider to every other sephiroth, and therefore mediates and transfers the divine energy throughout the universe. Indeed, Sallie Ann Glassman has given Silibo (called Shi-Li-Bo Nouvavou in her text) the place of the Six of Water in *the New Orleans Voodoo Tarot*, thus highlighting her qualities as the watery, nurturing, flowing force of

---

40 Fleurent, Gerdés. Dancing Spirits: Rhythms and rituals of Haitian Vodou, the Rada Rite, pp. 88.
41 Fleurent, Gerdés. Dancing Spirits: Rhythms and rituals of Haitian Vodou, the Rada Rite, pp. 88.
42 Rigaud, Milo. Ve-ve, pp. 96.

Tiphereth (the sixth sephiroth.)[43] Silibo, in my view, can be seen as a lwa who draws down the divine light of the sun and all its life-giving force to the earth and humankind, both physically and in a spiritual sense. Like the stream carries rich silt to the river mouth, Silibo carries the sun's spiritual force to all who are open to it.

Ogou Yamsan and Ogou Balendjo

The nation of spirits known as Nago contains a large number of spirits renowned as warrior spirits. From the machete-wielding Ogou Feray and the diplomat general Ogou Badagris, to the once-human rebel leader Genéral Dessalines, and the Yoruba-derived Ogou Chango and Ogou Batala, these spirits represent power, struggle, battle, and strength in its many forms. Many of the Ogou spirits are derived from older deities that worked the forge and shaped iron into weaponry, and thus it is natural to think of these spirits as associated with the element of fire. However, there are two spirits in this family who work on Agwe's ship and are therefore a part of his entourage as well: the brothers Ogou Yamsan and Ogou Balendjo.

Ogou Balendjo is said to be captain of Agwe's ship, and is often imagined as an older man who is quite peaceful and wise. When he comes in possession he does not talk much, but what he does say is of vast importance and aid to those around. He can best be described as the field medic of the Nago nation. Alongside the other Ogous he will take his place in battle and in a struggle, but use his power to heal the injured. He does not wield the machete but instead the surgeon's knife, and his methods of healing are nothing like those we usually associate with water! He cuts to the core of an issue, removing what is harmful or no longer needed. This is sometimes a painful process, but a necessary one. When I imagine Ogou Balendjo I see him on his knees in the mud of a battlefield, amputating a ruined arm with three quick and precise slices (a technique developed in World War I to minimise damage, pain, and time.) However, he is also known for making people better who are sick, ill, or poisoned, and thereby he also takes on the traditional role of a more watery, gentle healer. One song for him says:

---

43 Glassman, Sallie Ann, and Martinié, Louis. The New Orleans Voodoo Tarot, pp. 145-6.

Ogou Balendjo-o,	Oh, Ogou Balendjo
Se ou menm kap leve moun	It's you who picks people up
Le moun kap tonbe	When people are bound to fall
Se ou menm kap leve moun	It's you who picks people up
Le moun kap tonbe	When people are bound to fall
Le moun malad	When people are sick
Le moun manje pwason	When people are poisoned
O-Ogou Balendjo	Oh, Ogou Balendjo
Se ou menm kap leve moun	It's you who picks people up
Le moun kap tonbe	When people are bound to fall.[44]

In direct contrast to this sober, responsible spirit is his brother, Ogou Yamsan, who could best be described as a drunken sailor! Often a destructive lwa, he is imagined as a drunkard always with a bottle of rum in his hand, although he is still described in the following song as a hard worker, a particular attribute of all Ogou spirits. Evidently, his inebriation has little effect on his power:

Ogou Yamsan ki travay di	Ogou Yamsan works very hard
Ogou Yamsan gen boutey nan menm li	Ogou Yamsan has a bottle in his hand
Yamsan mache vit	Yamsan walks quickly
Le'l vini, tout sa la kay tonbe	When he comes everything inside the house falls over.[45]

Other Water Spirits

There are several spirits not mentioned here that are worth discussing briefly. They all form a part of Agwe's entourage, or are inextricably linked with the other water spirits.

First is Klemezine Klemey, mentioned above as Agwe's sister, who is to a greater or lesser extent depending on the tradition, another form of St. Claire. Usually seen as a spirit who grants clear vision, prophesy, and the ability to see truth in falsehood, she is another spirit who brings with her purity, cleanliness and healing.

---

[44] Taught at a workshop given by Papa Hector Salva of the Sosyete Gade Nou Leve, September 2009. Any mistakes in translation or Creole spelling are my own!
[45] As above footnote. Once again, any mistakes are my own.

Familial relations are rife in Vodou cosmology – many of the lwa have other lwa as children, partners, lovers, parents, siblings and cousins. Often a parent of many lwa or a family of lwa will have their name prefixed with the title of *'Gran'* indicating *'big'* or *'great'*. All the Simbis are related to Gran Simba, for instance, and in this case many of the female water spirits are daughters of a spirit named Gran Aloumba, herself a water spirit. However, whereas many of her water spirit daughters are pure and chaste, Gran Aloumba is highly sexual, taking many lovers. Depicted as an older woman in her 60's or 70's, she is still voluptuous and beautiful, confident in herself and her beauty, and with a sweet, friendly demeanour that can become assertive and direct if she is challenged. Whereas some water spirits, especially the female ones, are stereotyped as gentle and calm, and in some cases are completely de-sexualised, Gran Aloumba has retained her obvious sexuality. In my experience she reflects the enticement of the rolling waves and the pull humankind feels towards the ocean as Mother.

Mambo Lovanah is another spirit about whom little is written, though her title as Mambo indicates she is an extremely powerful lwa to work with. One of the many daughters of Gran Aloumba, Lovanah is imagined as a teenage girl, beautiful and fair, singing whilst she washes clothes in a river. Whereas most spirits eat offerings of food or drink, Lovanah survives only on the scent of fresh flowers. She is a spirit of cleansing and purity, along with many of the other spirits associated with water, and she is often gifted delicate perfumes, soaps, washing implements, and song.

Other spirits that are associated with water can be found outside of Agwe's entourage, and some are not often served but instead only mentioned out of respect during a Vodou ceremony. The spirits Sobo and Bade are brothers, and are depicted as the thunderstorm and the wind respectively. They may be called upon in times of drought, but otherwise they rarely interact with humans.

Themes and Conclusions

It would be interesting to study the implications of certain features found predominantly in these water spirits, such as that of being associated with purity, cleansing, sensuality, and healing. It would also raise some useful questions about the role water plays in the Vodou imagination and universe; some of these issues have been discussed briefly in this paper, but further discussion is not possible due to space. However, what is clear is that the element of water, and the spirits that inhabit and are associated with it, are vital to the Vodou religion, playing the role of psychopomp, healer, channel, nurturer, and acting as a painful reminder of the oppressive origins of the religion via the slave trade. Water, paradoxically, is seen as a means by which the religion came into being and therefore a point of origin through suffering, as well as a gateway through which the soul can return to a purer and more holistic state of being through relationship with God and the lwa.

Bibliography

Brown, Kathy. *Mama Lola: Vodou Priestess in Brooklyn.* University of California Press, 1991.
Crosley, M.D., Reginald. *The Vodou Quantum Leap: Alternate Realities, Power and Mysticism.* St Paul., Minnesota: Llewellyn Publications, 2000.
Courlander, *Gods of the Haitian Mountains.* . *The Journal of Negro History,* vol. 29, no. 3, (July 1944), pp. 339-372.
Deren, Maya. *Divine Horsemen: The Living Gods of Haiti.* McPherson and Company, 2004.
Filan, Kenaz. *The Haitian Vodou Handbook: Protocols for Riding with the Lwa.* Rochester, Vermont: Destiny Books, 2007.
Fleurent, Gerdés. *Dancing Spirits: Rhythms and rituals of Haitian Vodou, the Rada Rite.* Greenwood Press, 1996.
Glassman, Sallie Ann, and Martinié, Louis. *The New Orleans Voodoo Tarot.* Rochester, Vermont: Destiny Books, 1992.
Herskowitz, Melville. *African Gods and Catholic Saints in New World Negro Belief. American Anthropologist,* New Series, vol. 39, no. 4, Part 1 (Oct-Dec 1937), pp.635-643.
Lao, Meri. *Seduction and the Secret Power of Women: The Lure of Sirens and Mermaids.* Rochester, Vermont: Park Street Press, 2007.
Rigaud, Milo. *The Secrets of Voodoo.* City Lights Books, 1985.
Rigaud, Milo. *Vé-vé.* New York: French and European Publications, Inc., 1974.
Seabrook, William. *The Magic Island.* New York: Paragon House, 1989.
Simpson, George Eaton, *The Belief System of Haitian Vodun. American Anthropologist.* New Series, vol. 47, no. 1. (Jan.-March 1945), pp.35-59.

TO DARE

THE ELEMENT OF WATER IN THE WESTERN ESOTERIC TRADITIONS

BY SORITA D'ESTE

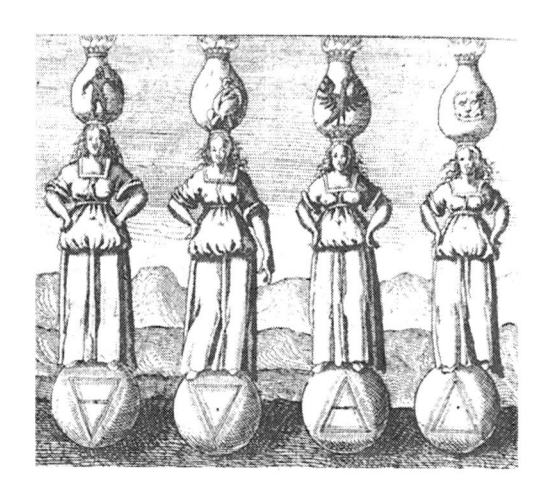

"For he hath given me certain knowledge of the things that are, namely, to know how the world was made, and the operation of the elements."
~ *The Wisdom of Solomon 7:17, C4th CE.*

The system of the four elements, Air, Fire, Water and Earth is a key foundation stone in the development of the Western Esoteric Tradition, and practices associated with it can still be found in almost all the modern traditions of magic and mysticism, including Alchemy, Gnosticism, Hermeticism, Ceremonial Magic, and Qabalah through to the Wiccan Tradition, Neo-Pagan Witchcraft and Druidry. Its historical origins can be found two and a half thousand years ago in the writings of the ancient Greek philosopher Empedocles. In the fifth century BCE in his *Tetrasomia (Doctrine of the Four Elements)*, Empedocles expressed the view that the four elements were not only the building blocks of the universe, but also spiritual essences. He equated the sources of the elements to Greek deities, thus attributing divine origins to the four elements.

> "Now hear the fourfold Roots of everything:
> Enlivening Hera, Aidoneus, bright Zeus,
> And Nestis, moistening mortal springs with tears."[46]

It is important however to note that Empedocles did not call his four principles *'elements'* (*stoikheia*), but rather he used the terms *'roots'* (*rhizai*) and *'root-clumps'* (*rhizômata*). Empedocles was an herbal magician or root cutter (*rhizotomoi*) and created his theory in the process of developing a doctrine of occult sympathies in plants. Notably, Empedocles' ideas were echoed a couple of hundred years later by the Ptolemaic Egyptian high priest and historian Manetho who recorded deity attributions which seem to provide a bridge between the ideas of Empedocles and that of later esoteric traditions, when he wrote:

> "The Egyptians say that Isis and Osiris are the Moon and the Sun; that Zeus is the name which they give to the all-pervading Spirit, Hephaestus to Fire, and Demeter to Earth. Among the Egyptians the moist element is named Oceanus and their own river Nile; and to him they ascribed the origin of the Gods. To Air, again, they give, it is said, the name of Athena."[47]

Empedocles' work was subsequently clarified and expanded on by many of the great philosophers and mystics whose work would subsequently influence the development of the western esoteric traditions through the centuries. These philosophers, mystics and magicians included luminaries such as Aristotle, Plato, Athenagoras, Aristides, Philolaos, Eusebius, Philo and Josephus.

> "Four phrases constitute and include all that is required for the possession of High Magical Power.
> To Know; To Dare; To Will; To Keep Silent."[48]

---

46 Tetrasomia, Empedocles, C5th BCE.
47 Manetho, Aegyptica Fragment 83, Waddell (trans), C2nd BCE.
48 Transcendental Magic by Eliphas Levi

The Four Directions

Today when we consider the four elements within western esotericism it is often in the context of the four directions, an idea which may have its origins in the writings of the Pythagorean philosopher Philolaos who wrote about the fourfold ordering of the elements in the context of the zodiacal circle. His system divided the zodiac into a circle with an equal armed cross, the symbol now used in the western esoteric tradition to represent the planet Earth. The Pythagoreans associated the elements with the natural cycle, tying the qualities of the elements to the seasons of plant growth. Thus we see the process beginning with *Moisture*, the spring rains which encourage rapid growth, producing the green shoots as plants grow towards the sun. This leads to the second phase of *Warmth*, where the summer sun encourages growth (through photosynthesis) to maturity. The third phase is *Dryness*, the leaves of autumn and the stiffening of stems. Finally the fourth phase is *Cool*, the chills of winter, death and retreat into the earth ready for the cycle to begin again. The attribution of the four elements to the four cardinal points can also be found in the writings of the Greek spiritual alchemist Zosimos of Panopolis who attributed the elements to the four cardinal points in his classic third century CE work *Upon the Letter Omega*.

Interestingly, the attribution of the four elements to the four directions remained constant for many centuries, being as follows:

East	Fire
South	Air
West	Water
North	Earth

Those readers familiar with the attributions most popular within western esotericism today will notice that these attributions are different from those generally used today. Yet examples of the above attributions can still be found in general use as recently as the late eighteenth century, as the following example from a *Key of Solomon* illustrates:

> "*the spirits created of fire are in the East and those of the winds in the South.*"[49]

---

49 Key of Solomon (various MSS).

ELIPHAS LEVI, (1810-1875)

Surprisingly the attribution of Fire to the South and Air to the East seems to originate with the nineteenth century occultist Eliphas Levi, whose work was hugely influential (yet often remains unaccredited) in the work of later magical societies, including that of the late nineteenth century Hermetic Order of the Golden Dawn. It was the use of Levi's attributions into the ceremonies of the Golden Dawn which would subsequently influence the attributions most often found in modern traditions, being:

East	Air
South	Fire
West	Water
North	Earth

Elemental Symbols

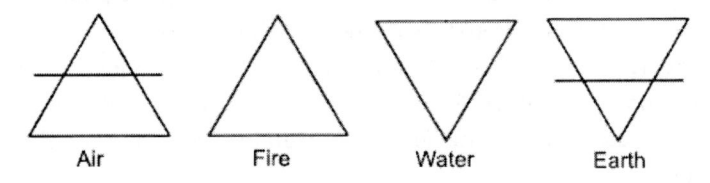

Air   Fire   Water   Earth

Before we consider the Element of Water in more detail, I feel it necessary to also briefly discuss the elemental symbols which are frequently used today to represent the elements. When overlapped, they form a hexagram, a symbol which is used for the universe which is apt as the four elements are considered to be the building blocks of the physical world, as well as the spiritual realms.

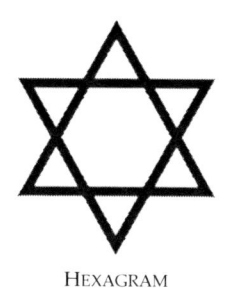

HEXAGRAM

The elements of Air and Fire are both represented by an upward pointing triangle, which represents their expansive (warm) nature. The upward triangle also symbolises the male phallus. The bar on the air triangle demonstrates that it is a denser element than fire. And Water and Earth are both represented by a downward pointing triangle, which represents their contractive (cool) nature. The downward triangle symbolises the female pubic triangle (i.e. genitalia). The bar on the earth triangle demonstrates that it is a denser element than water.

During the Middle Ages and Renaissance a whole range of symbols were used to represent water, as can be seen in the following image (taken from *Dictionary of Occult, Hermetic & Alchemical Sigils* by Fred Gettings, 1981). It is worth noting that Gettings emphasises the wavy lines used for water in ancient Egypt, which has been used as a convention for illustrations of water ever since.

> "Sublime waters ... which flow in their place, abundant waters which dwell together permanently in the great reservoir, children of the ocean which are seven, the waters are sublime, the waters are brilliantly pure, the waters glisten."[50]

The following tables contain some key examples of symbols and sigils used to represent water in different religious, magical and alchemical manuscripts as collected by Fred Gettings for his *Dictionary of Occult, Hermetic & Alchemical Sigils,* I have reproduced these symbols for this essays as the book is at the time of writing very rare and difficult to obtain.

---

50 Babylonian Hymn to the Waters, given in Chaldean Magic, Lenormant.

〰〰〰	Ancient Egyptian
⨯ over ▽	Berthelot 1885, from the Greek Alchemical Tradition
△ with dot on top	Shepherd 1971, from 14C
(symbol)	Agrippa 1510, for the Water Triplicity
▽ ~~~	Sloane MS 836, 1650
▽ ⋀⋀⋀	Crollius 1670
▽ ♈	Valentine 1671, Water of Life
〰〰	Fresne 1688
▽ with dot, ⋀⋀⋀, ∀	Edinburgh MS Adv. 23.1.10 17C
	Water of Life

Sigils for the Element of Water - Part 1

72 | From a Drop of Water

Symbols	Label
	Signa 17C
	Sommerhoff 1701
	Water of Life
	Rain Water
	Welling 1735 Invisible Spiritual Water

Sigils for the Element of Water - Part 2

73 | From a Drop of Water

〰 ☿	DIDEROT 1763
◁ ↑	WATER OF LIFE
∽C 〰	COMMON WATER
▽	GEHEIME 1785
▼ ↓	GESSMANN 1906
▽ ▽ ▽	RAIN WATER
▽	HOT WATER
∇enis ⊞ ∽∽nis	COMMON WATER
	UNSAVOURY WATER
)	CARBONELLI 1925
🐘	SHEPHERD 1971 QABALISTIC WATER

SIGILS FOR THE ELEMENT OF WATER - PART 3

74 | From a Drop of Water

Another practice found in traditions such as Ceremonial Magic and Wicca, is that of using the pentagram to represent the four elements, which combine to create the fifth, that of Spirit. Each point on the pentagram is thus attributed to one of the elements, with the topmost point being attributed to Spirit.

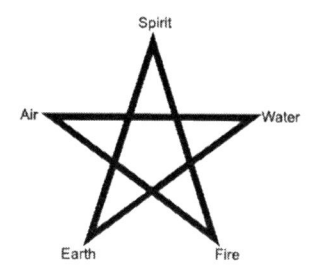

In practice these attributions are used in blessings and consecrations, as well as for creating sigils and talismans. Most often the pentagram is traced, in a particular sequence, to evoke the power of a particular element.

Invoking & Banishing Elemental Pentagrams

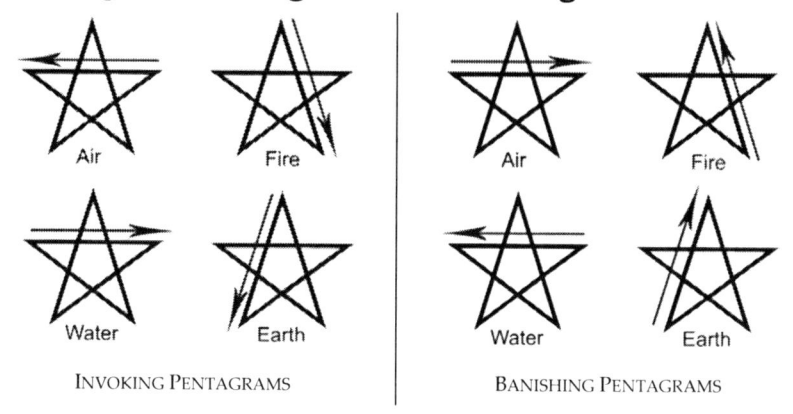

INVOKING PENTAGRAMS | BANISHING PENTAGRAMS

These magical gestures are used repeatedly and build up a power for the magician using them, as well as tapping into the energy already generated by it over the course of time by other magicians. Magic is described as many things by many different people and at different times, I quite like the definition which was given by the American occultist Pascal B Randolph (1825-1875), whose writings would subsequently influence Aleister Crowley and many others, in his work *Magia Sexualis* he wrote saying that:

> "Magick is a science. It is the only science which occupies itself, theoretically and practically, with the highest forces of nature, which are occult."

In addition to the uses already named, another very important use for the elemental pentagrams are in practices where the Guardians of the Four Cardinal directions are invoked. This practice is found in many traditions of Ceremonial Magic, and is also an essential part of traditions such as Wicca. From these traditions it has filtered down into a number of other NeoPagan traditions, though the use of the elemental pentagrams has sometimes been discarded. Their use is accompanied by visualisations, often the magician sees the pentagram forming as he traces it in the air in front of himself, sometimes in gold or in the appropriate elemental colour. For Water this would be blue.

Elemental Landscape of Water

Another use is that of exploring the Elemental Landscapes. These landscapes are essentially composed of features which epitomises the element it represents. If you plan on working with the elements in your own magical practices, or wish to further explore the element of Water within your existing practices, a simple, yet effective practice to incorporate into a ceremony is to draw the elemental invoking pentagram of Water, seeing the lines form as beautiful bright blue as you trace it. Then take a deep breath and trace the elemental symbol for Water in the centre of your pentagram, and allow yourself to enter into a meditative state during which you enter into the elemental landscape of Water. This is most often seen as follows:

> *"The Water landscape is a coastline. A river runs over a cliff, forming a waterfall down into the sea below, which ebbs and flows with its tides. On the beach below you can see rocks partially covered with seaweed waiting for the tide to come fully back in. In the water you may see creatures like dolphins and whales, fish and seals, as well as mythical creatures like mermaids and sea goats."*
>
> [From Circle of Fire, Sorita d'Este & David Rankine, Avalonia 2008 edition]

Of course you may find that you encounter the landscape in a different way, this is fine and in fact possibly a sign that you are doing things correctly!

Understand the mutability of Water

The Element of Water can change state of being in a more tangible and noticeable form than any of the other elements. A little exercise I like doing with individuals who are first seeking to understand the four elements is to get them to contemplate on each element in turn, with it physically present before them. For the Element of Water I have often used the following contemplation, it is one which David Rankine and I have frequently used with students over the years:

Ice Cube Meditation

For this meditation you need a bowl of water and an ice cube.

Place the bowl on the floor and sit comfortably gazing into it. Add the ice cube and watch it float around on the surface as it slowly melts. Consider how it moves and changes state, from solid to liquid, and contemplate the power of water in nature all around you, and how it exists as solid (ice), liquid (water) and gas (water vapour). Spend a few minutes doing this, or until the ice cube melts.

When you have finished, record your thoughts and observations.

The Correspondences of The Element of Water

All four the elements have both positive and negative qualities associated with them in a metaphysical context. The positive qualities of Water include *Compassion, Dreams, Emotions, Empathy, Nurturing, Psychism, Serenity, Sexuality, Sympathy* and *Trust.* The negative qualities being *Deceit, Fear, Hatred, Jealousy, Sorrow, Spite* and *Treachery.* The axiom given to Water in western magic today is *To Dare,* which is a necessary ability for us to develop if we are to control our emotions, whilst also enabling us to push the boundaries of our own personal experience and learning. All of which is important part of exploring the mysteries.

Water (aqua) is described by the alchemical acronym Aqua - *Album Quæ Vehit Aurum,* meaning *"Which Bears the White Gold."* The term white gold was used to describe liquid Mercury, also called the Water of the Philosophers.

There are multiple layers of symbolism and associations to explore when studying and exploring the element of Water, the following table of correspondences will provide the eager student with starting points for their own research and studies. It includes references to some of the spiritual beings which are associated with this element, which is an area of study which falls outside the scope of this essay, but one which is essential to the study of western mysticism and magic.

Axiom	To Dare
Colour (Modern)	Blue
Astrological Signs	Cancer, Pisces, Scorpio
Planets	Jupiter*, Moon (Neptune)
Direction	West
Time of Day	Dusk
Season	Autumn
Sense	Taste
Gender	Feminine
Tools	Cup
Deities	Persephone (Nestis), Poseidon
Tetragrammaton	Heh
Archangel	Gabriel
Demon King	Ariton
Enochian King	Raagiosel
Enochian Divine Name	Empeh Arsel Gaiol
Elemental Governor	Tharsis
Elemental King	Niksa
Elementals	Undines
Kerub	Man
Gem	Sapphire
Metal	Mercury
Tarot	Cups

The Life Giving Waters

The element of Water is the one which is most often associated with the primal creation, the origins of mankind and all life upon this Earth itself. It permeates the creation myths of many cultures, and is a primordial and powerful symbol of life. It is key in the Sumerian creation myth where the divine couple, Apsu and Tiamat, represents sweet water and salt water, the waters of the abyss.

The Egyptian Ogdoad, of four primal divine couples, likewise focused on the *Nun* or primal waters. This idea of the primal waters as the foundation of creation is also found in the work of Thales of Miletius, the seventh century BCE philosopher who is considered the first of the Greek philosophers. The idea continues on in the work of many thinkers, including the thirteenth century Kabbalist Azriel of Gerona who eloquently described water as the primeval mother who gave birth to darkness.

A concept frequently found in the grimoires, which has its origins in the Qabalah is that of *'Living Water'*, which is water which has fallen as rain or which has been drawn from a natural source such as a spring, or from lakes, ponds and rivers. It is pure water, as it has fallen from heaven. The importance of living water continues through into instructions found in grimoires such as the *Key of Solomon* for the magician to bathe in a river or similar source of living water. It may also be used for purifying ritual items, and in talismanic magick. This is why dew is sometimes associated with the highest Sephira of Kether in Kabbalistic texts as living water. This use of living water is also found in numerous native magical traditions in Europe and Britain which survive through to the modern day.

Water is a dichotomy. Life began in the waters. Water is vital for life, and like the element of Fire it can be both nurturing and destructive. In the macrocosm Water surrounds us as rain, rivers, lakes and oceans, it covers most of the planet we live on and it makes up the bulk of our bodies. The seas move in tides, reflecting our lives, which ebb and flow symbolically like the tides of the oceans. This struggle of water was expressed superbly by the Greek philosopher Heraclitus in the sixth century BCE when he wrote:

> "The sea is the purest and foulest water: for fish drinkable and life-sustaining; for men undrinkable and deadly."[51]

Of course, it is also true the other way around. The pure water of a river or lake would be poison to sea creatures, whilst it is sustains man and many other creatures.

Water can be nurturing, the *'waters of life'*, or it can symbolise death, the journey beyond the physical into the unknown, which has always been represented as a journey over water. The ancient Egyptian underworld, Amenti, was believed to be on the west of the river Nile, and the Celts saw the Isles of the Blessed (afterlife) as being in the west over the Atlantic Ocean. Such worldviews show that the link between water and the direction of the west has been symbolically present for thousands of years. Water additionally represents rebirth as well as death, and the compassion that comes from accepting inevitable change and encompassing it.

Working with the element of Water helps you to concentrate on harmonising your emotional being. Water can help you to both enhance positive emotional states like compassion, serenity and nurturing, as well as transforming negative states like deceit, jealousy, spite and treachery. Water can also help you focus on your subtle senses, developing your empathy and psychism, and working with your dreams.

Undines & the Elementals of Water

The concept of *'elementals'* is often quite misunderstood and, within modern magical traditions have become confused with a number of other concepts, including thought-forms and elementaries. When using the term I refer to the beings that are associated with a particular element, these are Sylphs for Air, Salamandars for Fire, Undines for Water and Gnomes for Earth. The concept of Water elementals is a very ancient one, Heraclitus wrote about it in the 6th century BCE saying:

> *"There are certain Water Elementals whom Orpheus calls Nereides, dwelling in the more elevated exhalations of Water,*
>
> *such as appear in damp, cloudy Air, whose bodies are sometimes seen (as Zoroaster taught) by more acute eyes, especially in Persia and Africa."*[52]

The name *'undine'* which we use for the elementals of Water is derived from the Latin word *unda*, meaning *'wave'*. In appearance Undines are said to appear with the same stature as a woman and are described as always appearing with moisture in their presence, which may manifest in many different ways such as for example, a sweat or a humid atmosphere. They are sometimes (incorrectly) referred to as *'Ondines'*, which is a similar sounding name of a specific water nymph in German mythology, whereas *'Undines'* refer to the whole class of being . Undines were particularly noted for marrying humans and bearing children to their husbands, in fact of all the elemental beings they are the most likely to engage in this pursuit! Unfortunately, this

---

51 Fragments, Heraclitus, C6th BCE.
52 Chaldean Oracles of Zoroaster, No.77.

inclination of theirs also frequently encapsulates their most tragic natures, as it seems to inevitably end in disaster.

One such example can be found in the hugely popular story of Melusine who was described in the late fourteenth century tale of *Mélusine de Lusignan*.[53] Melusine can be seen as the archetypal fairy wife, and appears in different versions of the story as half fish, serpent or dragon – all clearly illustrating her watery nature. She marries a man called Remond, who became the Conte de Poitiers, but with the caveat that on each and every Saturday he would allow her complete privacy. Melusine brings Remond great prosperity, she builds the fortress at Lusignan for him with great speed and ease, so much so that it appears to be by magic. Remond fails in this promise he made to Melusine after a visit by his brother who evokes feelings of jealousy in him about what Melusine does on a Saturday. As a result, he waits until the next Saturday and bursts in on her, finding her in a bath of water in her elemental shape and at once realises her true nature. She then leaves in a dramatic gesture, with Remond regretting his actions and mourning for her the rest of his life. She does make appearances to visit her children and subsequent generations of her downline, who are said to include the Kings of Cyprus, Armenia, Bohemia and the Duke of Luxembourg, as well as of course the Lord of Lusignan.

Reflecting on the tendency for female undines to marry male humans, De Villars comments, saying:

> "The ancient Sages called this race of people Undines or Nymphs. There are very few males among them but a great number of females; their beauty is extreme, and the daughters of men are not to be compared to them."[54]

As can be seen in this quote, Undines are also known as Nymphs a term which links back to a huge range of beings in the ancient world, Nymphs being particular popular in the mythologies of ancient Greece and Rome, as well as in the Romano-Celtic world.

Living Water Meditation

The following meditation is taken from the book *Practical Elemental Magick* (Avalonia, 2009) which I co-authored with David Rankine. It is a very simple, but useful practice to perform on a regular basis in order

---

53 Mélusine de Lusignan, Jean d'Arras, 1393

to explore the symbolism and qualities of the element of Water, especially if you are able to perform it as a regular outdoor practice by a stream or other natural body of water.

'Living Water' (*mayim hayim*) is water which has fallen from the sky bringing the purity of heaven with it, and has not been drawn from its source by pipes or a human hand. Living water is found in lakes, ponds, rivers and springs, and may be collected as dew by leaving a bowl out overnight during the appropriate seasons. By the definition this is not something that would really fit with acid rain in a big city, which would not perhaps be living water in the same way as was originally meant. However if you can go and visit a suitable site in the countryside and collect water from a spring or overnight dew, you can use it for magickal work and meditation. To gather water not by hand, put a bowl in the water so it is filled by the water, and then extricate it, so it has not strictly speaking been gathered by a human hand. If you do go to a spring, then that is a preferable site for the following meditation, rather than at home.

Sit next to the water (be it a pool, spring, bowl, etc) and watch the surface of the water. Consider how this water is living water, which has been transformed into vapour, and possibly also into ice. It has experienced many changes of state, and will experience more, for water is a medium of transformation, going through change and also creating change.

Place your face as close as you conveniently (and safely) can to the water and say your magickal name over the surface of the water. (This is an old Qabalistic practice, of only speaking words of power over water, probably based on *Genesis 1:2*). Watch the surface of the water to see if it is moved by your breath, and see the small ripples spread, showing how a simple act can have repercussions which continue for a long time afterwards.

As you gaze at the water, you feel its still, mirror-like surface calm you, and you recall how the practice of hydromancy, or water divination, was used in ancient times to

---

54 Le Comte de Gabalis, de Villars, 1670.

see spiritual creatures and other places. As you look at the living water, you start to be aware that it is also a gateway of possibility. Allow yourself to see any visions which may unfold, but if they do not, be aware that some of the living water is evaporating and surrounding you as you gaze. Dip a fingertip into the water and anoint your brow with the water. Repeat this for your eyelids, and then drop a drop of the water into your mouth. Be aware of the power contained within even the smallest drop of water, and how it can be used to purify and also open doorways for you.

With its ability to exist in different states, and it association with the emotions, dreams, the unconscious, the otherworld and the lower astral realms, water may be seen in many ways as the most challenging of the elements. From a drop of rain to a tsunami, the power of water to bring change is ever-present, and it is how we deal with that change which measures whether we harness the tide or are blown about like driftwood. For a magician in the western esoteric traditions, the emphasis is on going with the tides, or learning to control them, and to do this we need to come to terms with water and accept it as a major part of our being.

Further Reading:

Ashe, Steven (ed), *The Testament of Solomon & The Wisdom of Solomon*, 2008, Glastonbury Books, Glastonbury
De Villars, Monfaucon, *The Count de Gabalis*, 1714 (English translation of the 1670 French work), B.Lintott & E. Curll, London
Gettings, Fred, *Dictionary of Occult, Hermetic & Alchemical Sigils*, 1981, Routledge and Kegan Paul, London
Kingsley, Peter, *Ancient Philosophy, Mystery and Magic; Empedocles and the Pythagorean Tradition*, 1995, Oxford University Press, Oxford
Kirk, G. S., Raven, J. E. & Schofield, M., *The Presocratic Philosophers*, 1983, Cambridge University Press, Cambridge
Lenormant, Francois, *Chaldean Magic: Its Origin and Development*, 1999 (first published 1878), Red Wheel Weiser, Maine
Levi, Eliphas, *Transcendental Magic*, 1979, Rider & Co, London
Randolph, Pascal B., *Magia Sexualis*, 1987 (first published in French as *Eulis* in 1876), Ediz Mediterranee, Rome
Rankine, David & d'Este, Sorita, *Practical Elemental Magick*, 2009, Avalonia, London
Rankine, David & d'Este, Sorita, *Practical Planetary Magick*, 2007, Avalonia, London
Rankine, David & d'Este, Sorita, *Practical Qabalistic Magick*, 2009, Avalonia, London
Rankine, David & d'Este, Sorita, *Wicca Magickal Beginnings*, 2008, Avalonia, London

THE WELL SPRING OF WISDOM

SACRED WELLS IN FAITH THROUGH THE AGES

BY KATHERINE SUTHERLAND

How like a womb this Well is,
nestling quietly beneath the mounds
of moss and turf, dying tissue, shrinking
from the light, hides your ghost worn gleam
of essence.

Within your body, a gentle power, momentarily
lost in the void that we all reach out to touch,
and I reach over that yawning precipice,
to trust and fall again, into your waiting arms

Water is vital to humanity: the Greek philosopher Thales stated his belief that it is the original stuff from which all else is formed, and that the earth rests on water. Later Leonardo Da Vinci wrote of water and its changing nature:

"It has nothing of its own but takes everything, changing into as many different natures as there are difference places on its course, acting just like a mirror, which takes in as many images as there are things passing in front of it."[55]

The human body is approximately 56% liquid, and water covers about three fifths of the entire surface of the earth. Scholars continue to demonstrate how concepts of fertility, nurture, relief and regeneration are popularly expressed through water imagery. Because it is indispensable for life, water has a natural capacity to extend metaphorically to encompass a range of human experiences and emotions; both on individual and community levels the study of water-based practices can teach us much about cultural values expressed in

---

[55] Richter, Jean Paul, ed. The Literary Works of Leonardo da Vinci, Vol 2, 3rd edition, London, Phaidon, 1970, p. 159.

relation to a basic natural element. There is a vast range of cultural assumptions pertaining to water, which are evidenced in major religions, hydro-mythology and the Christian church's accommodation and transformation of earlier customs; these can also be related to the rise of the spa industry and the rise of the bottled water industry to the present day.

Current folkloric thinking on holy wells and spas is often based upon the assumption of supernatural or religious associations that are thought to be extinct. Such age old ideas are present in the belief that water is healing, it can cure pain and disease, give longevity of life and serve as a medium for divinatory work. As late as the sixteenth century, the holy well was to be found at the centre of annual religious rites, such as pilgrimage, well dressing, and the placement of votive offerings. Such sites often featured both in the legends of Christian saints, and in local folk legends of otherworldly events. However, as Church reform introduced new attitudes, the practices surrounding holy wells flowed into two streams; the wells being relegated to the realm of superstition and the water being ascribed the profane powers of the rational world.

As ideas shifted with the Reformation and Enlightenment, and dialectic notions of the *'noble savage'* came to the fore, water became a significant focal point for a belief system unencumbered by scientific discoveries that were rising to challenge its precedence. Pierre Perrault's *Treatise on the Origins of Springs*,[56] presented in Paris in 1674, changed scientific thinking on water. Perrault suggested that waters that fall to earth are the origins of springs, challenging the centuries-old view that water was produced by underground powers. This new position contrasted with a long line of thinkers, including Plato, Aristotle and St. Thomas Aquinas whom had all believed that underground reservoirs feed the earth. Perrault therefore provided a further assault in the battle against traditional beliefs about water. In this battle, church authorities did attempt to purge water beliefs and practices, which were viewed as idolatry, throughout the seventeenth century. However, although these efforts were not entirely successful, they did create a stream with dual flow, which is reflected in contemporary approaches to holy wells, the rise of the spa and the power of the bottled water industry. The sacred views of water as

---

[56] For further details of Perrault's work with water see: Hydrology: An Introduction, by Wilfried Brutsaert, Cambridge University Press, Cambridge 1996, pp. 573-581

possessing healing properties can be seen as the sacred counterparts of the claims of modern mineral water companies. Thus, the symbolic role of water in a modern secular society is best understood in the context of religious scriptures that preceded the current position it occupies.

In both Western and Eastern scriptures, the image of water is abundant. Water is referred to in spiritual and temporal life giving terms. Water is baptismal, present in fountains and in depths, in peace pools and as a place of residence of the divine feminine. Rainfall is seen as a symbolic outpouring of wisdom realised in a literal way; rivers are symbolic of the evolutionary course of the world soul, and thirst is seen as a longing for divine truth. In baptism, water cleanses the stains of perceived original sin; water allows the symbolic purification of the soul by its truth. Fountains are seen as outpouring of truth from above, *'For with thee is the fountain of life'*,[57] and in the Hindu faith, as saliva falls from the mouth of Dharma, water springs up upon the earth. Bathing and immersion in holy water at sacred sites is symbolic of the achievement of heightened states of consciousness and aspirational connections with the divine. Principal rivers of countries are often viewed as sacred, the Nile, the Ganges, the Shannon, and rivers are seen as symbolic of divine life flowing throughout the land. Through these brief references to scripture, it can be seen that water has a pre-eminent role in the poetic expression of spiritual beliefs and this storehouse of imagery has had a profound effect on the ways in which modern experiences with water are expressed.

Many have written about the lore of water as a simple and natural phenomenon; an element which will retain its power when reverence for all other concepts of divinity are forgotten. When other trappings fade, the primitive powers of cleansing, healing, and atoning remain. Historical sources document the appearance of springs at a Saint's pleasure or at other auspicious times. Folklore suggests curative and youth giving properties or conversely warning which are documented in many Scottish and English popular ballads, in which the holy well becomes a place of enchantment and spells and baptism and holy water become agents with which to counteract such preternatural encounters. Many murder scenes in ballads happen in proximity to wells; they are also ideal locations for fairy capture to take place. The motif of the well as the place of encounter survives in modern times, yet

---

57 Psalms 36:10

early Irish literature provides an excellent source of evidence regarding the centrality of the holy well to Celtic Pagan life.

Dindshenchas, a history of strongholds, takes the reader on a tour of ancient aristocratic Ireland. Beginning at the seat of the High Kings at Tara, three wells are mentioned: Nemnach, situated at a fairy mound and issuing forth a brook, the Caprach of Cormac, shaded by a majestic ash tree, and the wells of Adlaic or Di-Adlaic, which appear to be magical - one being benign, the other malignant. According to the poem, another important well exists on the mountains in County Sligo. Where *Dindshenchas* associates Tara with Kingship, Uisnech is linked with spirituality. Shrouded in the supernatural, this well is viewed as a source of inspiration and knowledge. The notion of twelve streams supposedly caused by a miracle endows the well with significance. Over it, nine sacred hazels grow, which hold knowledge within them. There is not scope in this article to further explore the depth of the extensive Irish associations with the holy nature of wells; yet the ideas of Kingship, feasting, storytelling, fecundity, wisdom, inspiration and the cult of the head appear in connection with wells in classical Irish literature.

In the process of Christianisation, many pre-Christian beliefs and customs relating to holy wells were adapted; hence a total rejection of old pagan gods was not demanded. Since wells provide a handy supply of water, many churches and religious houses were constructed in proximity to them, for example, Winchester Cathedral is built over the site of a pagan well, with its holy waters being converted for Christian use. Yet despite the prohibition of pagan worship at wells, it appears to have continued unabated. The initial attacks on well worship and practices centred on a dislike for magic and superstition. In the eighteenth century the direction of the attack changed, with the rise of scientific knowledge and the triumph of the rational; however the nineteenth century's observances of what it calls *'irreligious'* practices at holy wells have ironically served to perpetuate such customs. Modern rag tying, coin tossing and the leaving of offerings form part of the history of this complex ritual phenomenon.

It is clear that the power of water is often known intuitively by people who frequent wells and that attitudes and beliefs are often perpetuated through successive generations of community; acquiring embellishment, but often also retaining links to identifiable origins. It can be argued that belief that healing will occur is enough to ensure success for the modern water pilgrim. However, water is not an inert substance, possessing many measurable mineral qualities that create physical benefits when living water is taken. It is evident that many well rituals survive, and although these are patterned to suit the current dominant community beliefs, the links with the pagan past are often clearly visible. Evidence for modern water cults is scant, and the number of holy wells surviving in the British Isles is a fraction of the number that once existed. However, many modern festivals are constituted to involve the local holy well and custom of well dressing continues to be adopted. In the twenty-first century with the rise of concern for the environment and antiquities, I hope that restoration of holy wells will continue, as they form a valuable and little appreciated link to our pagan past.

The Wellspring of Healing ~ A modern take on old practice.

A Ceremony to kindle the well spring within our hearts, to offer healing to those in need and to celebrate the greening of the earth.

Parts
- Priestess & Priest to open and close the space
- Guardians of the directions, East, South, West and North
- Guardians of the centre of the circle, Above, Below and Within
- Guardian of the Holy Well
- Bride
- Bearers of Bride's Belt

Props
- Altar with appropriate incense burning
- A candle for each participant
- Cauldron
- A decorated hoop for the participants to pass through – Bride's belt / the well head
- A large white candle to be carried by Bride
- A veil for the oracular speaker
- Broomstick
- Music

Altar Layout

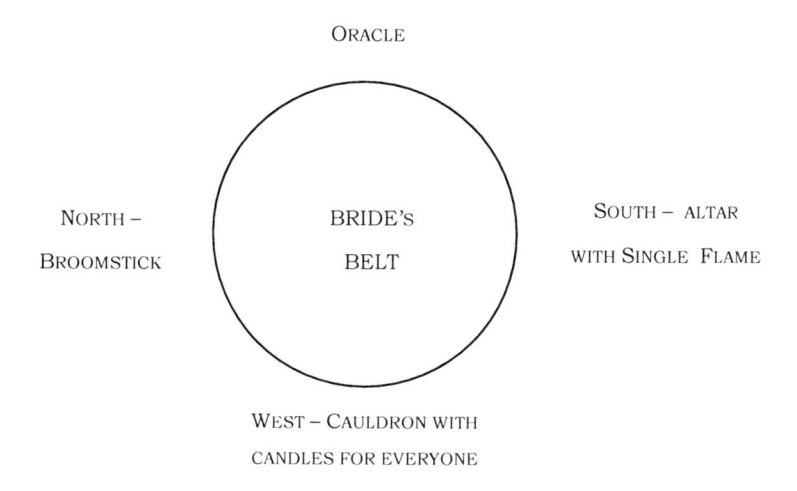

```
                    ORACLE

NORTH –          BRIDE'S          SOUTH – ALTAR
BROOMSTICK        BELT            WITH SINGLE FLAME

              WEST – CAULDRON WITH
              CANDLES FOR EVERYONE
```

The Opening

(Bride waits without to be called in)

Priestess and Priest: (Opening the sacred space with the intent of celebrating the festival of Bride and to kindle the well spring of our heart's desire.)

East: *In the place of new beginnings I summon Bride the healer, patroness of herbs and health I ask that your life giving power may be extended to this circle.*

South: *In the place of fire I summon Bride the bringer of greening for the land, patroness of the serpent power; I ask that your wisdom may be given to this circle.*

West: *In the place of flowing water I summon Bride the Bard, patroness of poets and teachers, I ask that your inspiration be shared with this circle.*

North: *In the place of the physical form I summon Bride the Smith, patroness of the forge; I ask that your protection be given to this circle.*

Above: (Opens in own words)

Below: (Opens in own words)

Within: (Opens in own words)

Calling in the Bride of Spring

North: *It is the time of new beginnings, a time for the dark chill of winter to retreat as the light returns; as the Cailleach departs let us silently thank the Goddess of winter for nurturing the seeds of our desire as they slept, dreaming in the cold and quiet earth.*

(Sweeps the circle anti clockwise with the broom)

East: *It is time to rekindle the flame of the wellspring, for the lady waits without. Let us open the door and let her in.*

(Lets Bride in at the East. Bride carries her candle around the circle clockwise, and then places it on the central altar; she then stands in the East.)

South: *Behold the Serpent Queen. Bride is come!*

All: *Bride is welcome!*

Empowering Bride's Belt

(The Bearers of Bride's Belt now place the hoop in the centre of the circle)

Bearers 1 & 2: *Behold the girdle of the goddess, the belt of Bride, the sacred well-head*

Bearer 1: *It is the time of renewal and healing and a time of new beginnings.*

Bearer 2: *Will you empower Bride's Belt with your tokens?*

(The company knots any tokens that they have brought onto the hoop in the centre; these will be returned at the end of the ceremony and can be used as objects of power throughout the year)

The Journey and Oracle

(Bride sits veiled in the East – Music One)

Guardian of the Well: *Think of yourself walking on a path on a warm spring day. The path is well worn and you already seem to know the way, and you feel as if you have walked here so many times before. You see before you lush green rolling hills and in the distance a large wooden bridge. As you continue to walk to notice that the path becomes a bit more steep and rocky, first going up and then going down the rolling hills. You exert yourself to walk the path but it feels good and you are enjoying the pace. As you continue to walk you notice that it is late afternoon and there is a slight breeze. It is quiet, except for the bleating of the sheep grazing nearby and the songs of small birds.*

You walk a bit faster now and the bridge is so close that you can see the wooden moss covered beams covering the bridge in a green and brown canopy. The bridge spans a small stream and hazel trees grow near the bridge. The gurgling and bubbling of the water feels relaxing. You stop on the bank to scoop up the cool clear water to drink. As you pause you see salmon and other fish swimming in the crystal clear stream. The sunlight glints on the water and catches your eyes. Take some time to rest from your long walk and enjoy the cool stillness of the bridge. Refreshed from your break you continue over the bridge into a dense forest filled with huge trees.

(Slight Pause)

You are not afraid as your feet move steadily along the thick carpet of leaves and moss. The vegetation is thick and sometimes the underbrush is thorny and scratches your legs. It is dark and hard to walk but your feet always seem to know the way. The smell is very earthy and very fresh and you breathe deeply. As you continue to move through the forest you hear people talking and laughing in the distance, the more you walk, the closer the sound gets.

(Slight Pause)

You soon start to see a light through the trees and the trees and undergrowth start to get thinner. As you walk on the path through the forest, you suddenly come into a clearing surrounded on one side by cliffs. You see men, women and children dressed in colourful clothing - the women have colourful wreaths of different types of flowers on their heads while the men are carrying flowering branches of apple, pear and other types of flowering plants. In front of you, at the base of the cliffs you see running water flowing into a round stone well and you are drawn towards it. One of the women walks up to you, gently takes your hand, leads you toward the well and says with a soft smile, "Welcome, we have been expecting you". As you get closer to the well, you notice that it has been decorated with beautiful flowers, seeds, branches leaves and shells. Much care has been taken in making the design with the natural materials..... "Go ahead", says the mysterious woman, "Look deep into the well...the well guardians have much to tell you". You walk around the well sun-wise three times and then you gaze deeply into the inky black depths of the well and the well reveals a vision for only you to see...

(Long Pause)

You walk back toward the forest and into the deep canopy of trees retracing your steps. The path seems easier now somehow and you make it easily through the forest. As you walk and retrace your steps you start to become aware of your physical feet. Listen to my voice. You become aware of a flicker of light, visible from the corner of your eye. As you make your way towards that flame you realize you are in the presence of a Goddess. Listen carefully to her words...

The Oracle of Bride (The company may sing / tone if they wish. Bride speaks as driven by spirit to do so.)

Guardian of the Well: *It is the time of return. Even though you may not want to return to the here and now, you must. You feel your feet and legs now and you are starting to become aware of things around you. You start to feel your physical body- you are aware of your own breathing. Your arms are feeling heavy and you can move them around if you want... wiggle your fingers and stretch. You feel the floor beneath you and when you feel that you are ready you can open your eyes...*

(Music two)

(The company sit in quiet contemplation as East and West unveil and ground Bride, the Bearers of Bride's Belt then present the hoop and the cauldron with the candles for her blessings, they return the hoop to the centre and the cauldron with the candles to the west.)

The Blessings

Bride: (Blesses the hoop and the candles in her own words)

Bearer 1: *It is time to emerge wide-eyed into the world!*

Bearer 2: *This is the girdle of the Goddess, the holy well head. Rise up company and pass through to receive the blessings of Bride.*

(The company led by Bride approach the hoop and pass through it three times by lifting it over their heads passing it over the body and stepping through, after the third time each member collects a candle from the cauldron in the west, lights it from the central candle on the altar then returns to their place in the circle.)

Bearer 1: *Let us now share the blessings and healings we have received within this circle with the wider circle of the earth.*

(All turn out and with lit candles send the blessings of the sacred flame of Bride to those in need – when finished blow out candles and turn to face inwards again)

The Communion

(Guardian of the Well and Bride bless the bread and spring water in their own words and take the communion around the assembled company)

The Closing

Above: (Closes in own words)

Below: *(Closes in own words)*

Within: (Closes in own words)

North: *In the place of the physical form I thank Bride the Smith, patroness of the forge; and I offer thanks for your protection that has been given to this circle.*

West: *In the place of flowing water I thank Bride the Bard, patroness of poets and teachers, I thank you for the inspiration that has been shared with this circle.*

South: *In the place of fire I thank Bride the bringer of greening for the land, patroness of the serpent power; I thank you for the wisdom that has been given to this circle.*

East: *In the place of new beginnings I thank Bride the healer, patroness of herbs and health I offer thanks for your life giving powers of renewal.*

Priestess and Priest: (Close the sacred space.)

Further Reading:

An electronic version of *Dindshenchas*, a history of strongholds, is available online, thanks to the work of the University of Cork:
http://www.ucc.ie/celt/published/T106500B/index.html

Further reading on holy wells is often geographically specific, with many titles available. For a more general overview of this area I would recommend:

Bord, Janet and Colin, *Sacred waters: holy wells and water lore in Britain and Ireland*. Paladin Books, 1986.
Bord, Janet, *Holy Wells of Britain*. Heart of Albion Press, Market Harborough 2008
Harte, Jeremy, *English Holy Wells: v. 1: A Sourcebook*. Heart of Albion Press, Market Harborough, 2008.
Rattue, James, *The Living Stream: Holy Wells in Historical Context*. The Boydell Press, Woodbrige, 2001.

A FLOW OF WATER THROUGH THE GRIMOIRE WORLD

EXPLORING HOLY WATER, CLEANSING BATHS AS WELL AS MAGICAL OPERATIONS LIKE THE WATER OF LIFE AND TURNING WATER IN TO BLOOD

BY MAESTRO NESTOR

First I would like to point out that this essay is written from a traditional grimoire magician's view, therefore we will explore the techniques and practices as they are in the grimoires, not adding or removing from them. In this essay I will explore the use of water in these grimoires for a wide variety of purposes. What strikes you first when you study the grimoires is the extensive use of holy water: you need it for performing all kinds of things. Cleansing baths are also a common in many of the grimoires. They prescribe that the magician repeatedly be bathing or washing himself, so it fits people that do not like to be dirty!

In the older[58] grimoires like the *6th and 7th Books of Moses* or the *Sword of Moses*, holy water is not used in the same way. Here we instead find how to perform many of the miracles that God and Moses performed, such as turning water into blood or creating floods like that of Noah.

In the so-called '*experiments*'[59] of the grimoires we see uses of other types of water, like rose water for example. Here we can also find procedures for how to make it rain and other interesting phenomena. The experiments of the grimoires are often overlooked but are a clear bridge between the grimoires and traditions of folk magic and witchcraft. David Rankine and Stephen Skinner released an interesting

---

[58] With older I refer to the legendary age and not the actual age of the documents we have found.
[59] Experiments in a grimoire refer to the parts that do not deal with the evocations. The evocation of a grimoire is usually its primary part but most grimoires also includes other magical operations that are often referred to as the experiments.

book concerning many of these overlooked experiments - *A Collection of Magical Secrets & A Treatise of Mixed Cabalah* - that I can highly recommend for people who wish to dig deeper into it.

Finally in the grimoires we also find the many different spirits that deal with or rule over water. They can often help the magician with safe passage over water, safe passage of goods over water, or to find the treasures of the deep. Most of these spirits are under the influence of the moon and it is even mentioned in *The Key of Solomon* that all operations regarding water should be made in the hours of the moon.[60]

What I find a bit surprising, however, is that there is hardly anything in them about finding water. It would be safe to assume that people living in the Middle East would be more concerned about this use of magical powers than those the grimoires prescribe.

Holy water

There are different kinds of holy water being used in the grimoires. *The Key of Solomon* for example describes in detail how to make the holy water that is to be used therein. This allows for a possibility that modern grimoire magicians have recently started discussing: when Skinner and Rankine did the research *for The Veritable Key of Solomon* they found an astonishing amount of different versions of the *Key of Solomon* in many different languages.[61] A theory many have drawn from this is the conclusion that perhaps the *Key of Solomon* was used as a primer[62] for earlier magicians. This means that later grimoires might have left some parts out regarding the more practical techniques such as the consecration of tools. This could mean that perhaps the later grimoires assumed we would use the descriptions on how to make the holy water from the *Key of Solomon*.

There are a few exceptions that can be seen in this theory. Those are the more Christian-based grimoires like the *Heptameron*[63] and the *Grimoire of Pope Honorius* (do not confuse this book with *the Sworn*

---

[60] See Key of Solomon book one page 14.
[61] For an exact number of manuscripts found and list of languages please see this article by David Rankine
http://grimoires.avalonia.co.uk/magic/greater_lesser_key.htm .
[62] See the following article for more information on this theory. Solomon's Keys: Revealing the Origins of Modern Ritual Practices by David Rankine at http://www.llewellynjournal.com/article/1871 .
[63] See Joseph Lisiewski's Ceremonial Magic & The Power of Evocation published by Original Falcon for a translation and instructions of the Heptameron.

Book of Honorius).[64] There it is obvious that the holy water we are talking about is the Catholic holy water: this is made clear in the texts that mention pure Catholic Masses and similar.[65]

If nothing else is said in a specific grimoire the water should preferably be taken from a spring or a fountain.[66] The symbolism of the fountain is a rather interesting alternative to the spring that is extremely evocative: both spring and fountain waters are moving waters, and moving water usually means that it is clean and pure. For a grimoire magician purity and cleanliness are crucial components for something to be considered holy. Fountains have existed for a very long time. They were frequently used by the Greeks in their major cities as early as 600 BCE.[67] It is also said that the ancient Egyptians had fountains but none of them are left today. So we can probably find support for the use of fountains even in Solomon's days. Fountains have been used for religious and ceremonial purposes for a long time. In later times it came to symbolize baptism and was known as the fountain of life. Another famous and mythical fountain is the fountain of youth. So we can clearly see the holy and religious aspects of a fountain. Another type of water worth mentioning is living water.[68] It is simply rain water and the theory is that since it comes from heaven it will have holy properties. It is often used in alchemical experiments. Because of recent pollution on can question how pure this water really is. Today, however, you can use tap water just as effectively: this is what I use and many priests I have spoken to use tap water also, but if you want to keep to the traditional ways you better go find a fountain for the base ingredient of your holy water.

The creation of holy water, no matter the source, is mainly a blessing of the water and salt and it is sometimes started with an

---

64 See the Grimoire of Honorius published by Trident Books. For a cheap but not as reliable translation you should check out Simon's Papal Magic: Occult Practices Within the Catholic Church published by Harper.
65 For example in Joseph Lisiewski's Ceremonial Magic & The Power of Evocation the mass of the holy ghost is mentioned on many occasions. In the Grimoire of Honorius it becomes very obvious that it's a catholic grimoire by quotes like this "In the name of the Father, of the Son, and of the Holy Spirit, of St. John the Baptist and of My Lord Abraham." The entire grimoire is written in that Christian manner.
66 In the Key of Solomon book two page 121 we can see that fountain water is used as sacrifice to the spirits. In the Grand Grimoire fountain water is a part of an experiment to make your self invisible. In the Sword of Moses you bath in a fountain as part of a ritual; see page 11.
67 For example Athens main fountain Enneacrounos around 6th century B.C.
68 See Practical Elemental Magick by David Rankine and Sorita d'Este page 44.

exorcism of the water and salt. The exorcism purifies it further and the blessing is what makes it holy. As already said there are some grimoires like the *Key of Solomon* that includes rites to make your holy water yourself in this way, so there is little problem acquiring the substance this way. Getting holy water or baptismal water from a Catholic Church can be more of a problem though. You could do as Dr Lisiewski recommends in his book *Ceremonial Magic & The Power of Evocation* and start to attend masses and baptisms and discretely take some water when no one is looking.[69] The holy waters that you can buy from different esoteric shops are not likely to be made by a Catholic priest either so I would not recommend using that. The best solution I think is to make the holy water yourself: that way you know it is being done the correct way. The actual ritual to create Catholic holy water is found in a book called the *Roman Ritual* or *Rituale Romanum*.[70] It contains many of the rituals a grimoire magician needs. In my opinion this is a book that all grimoire magicians should have in their library.

Some of you might foresee a problem here: that is that many of these rituals can only be performed by an ordained Catholic priest according to the Catholic Church and its rites. Now depending on how strict you are in your beliefs I can offer a solution to that. There is a passage in the Key of Solomon that I use as a way of explaining to God why I am doing certain rituals myself instead of letting a priest perform it:

> "ZAZAII, ZAMAII, PUIDAMON Most Powerful, SEDON Most Strong. EL, YODHE VAU HE, IAH, AGLA, assist me an unworthy sinner who have had the boldness to pronounce these Holy Names which no man should name and invoke save in very great danger. Therefor have recourse unto these Most Holy Names, being in great peril both of soul and of body. Pardon me if I have sinned in any manner, for I trust in Thy protection alone, especially on this journey."[71]

I read this before I do any of the rituals that normally demand ordained priesthood to let God know that I do not trust anyone else to do this for me and ask for his blessing in my work. This has worked for

---

69 See Joseph Lisiewski's Ceremonial Magic & The Power of Evocation page 149.
70 For a good translation see Philip T. Weller, Roman Ritual Volume 1-3, published by Preserving Christian Publications. It contains most of the Vatican approved masses, blessings and rituals that are used by their priesthood.
71 From The Greater Key of Solomon Book 2, pp. 96, trans. S.M.L Mathers.

me but we all need to decide what we feel is the best option that suits us and our purposes.

Let's take a look at how holy water is created in *The Key of Solomon*.

> "*After this thou shalt take a vessel of brass, of lead varnished within and without, or of earth, which thou shalt fill with most clear spring water, and thou shalt have salt, and say these words over the salt:*
>
> *TZABAOTH, MESSIACH, EMANUEL, ELOHIM GIBOR, YOD HE VAU HE: O God who art the Truth and the Life, deign to bless and sanctify this Creature of Salt, to serve unto us for help, protection, and assistance in this Art, experiment, and operation, and may it be a succor unto us. After this cast the salt into the vessel wherein is the Water, and say the following Psalms: cii.; liv.; vi.; lxvii.*"[72]

The catholic holy water is actually made in very similar way. The main difference being that it is a Christian ritual and the *Key of Solomon* is a Judaic ritual. In the *Rituale Romanum* they still use the two main ingredients of salt and water. One difference is that they also exorcise the water and salt before it is used.

This holy water is then used in a variety of ways in the grimoires. The main purpose is that of sprinkling it on items, places or people that need to be purified. Having a sprinkler is important for this. If you are using Catholic holy water you can buy a sprinkler from one of the many stores that sells supplies for Catholics. If you follow the *Key of Solomon* it is trickier: the sprinkler should be made of vervain, fennel, lavender, sage, valerian mint, garden-basil, rosemary, and hyssop. It should be collected in the day and hour of Mercury with the moon increasing. The herbs are then tied together by a thread spun by a young maiden. Finally you need to engrave each side of it with magical characters.[73]

People who claim magic is easy have probably never studied grimoire magic.

---

[72] From The Greater Key of Solomon book two page 107.
[73] For the characters see figure 82 and 83 in book two of the Greater Key of Solomon.

The Baths

As I mentioned in the Introduction baths are a frequent occurrence during the ritual preparations in the grimoires. There are a few reasons for this, becoming pure and clean being among of the most important reasons for having a bath. The whole idea of the preparation period is to become pure and clean both in mind and body. Water symbolizes purity and holiness in the grimoires and thus not only purifies the body but encourages a holy state of mind.

Another reason for the baths and why each day or major operation starts with cleaning yourself with water in one way or another is to let the magician and his eventual assistants step into the roles they play. It is a ritual action signifying that he is leaving his normal life and entering the life of a magician.

For this you use something like a tub of water, sometimes you just wash yourself from a bucket, other times you go to a river or spring and in some cases you use a fountain. This is usually described in each individual grimoire. If it is not I would recommend following the instructions in the *Key of Solomon*. An interesting note is that when it comes to the bathing water it self should also be exorcised which was not needed for the making the water of the art.[74]

In this example from the *Key of Solomon* we can clearly see the importance of being clean as well as how it prepares the magician to enter his role as a magician. Fittingly enough the part is called *"In What Manner the Master of the Art Should Keep, Rule, And Govern Himself"*.

> *"After this he must strip himself entirely naked, and let him have a bath ready prepared, wherein is water exorcised, after the manner which we shall describe, so that he may bathe and purify himself therein from the crown of his head unto the sole of his foot, saying: O Lord ADONAI, who hast formed me Thine unworthy servant in Thine Image and resemblance of vile and of abject earth; deign to bless and to sanctify this Water, so that it may be for the health and purification of my soul, and of my body, so that no foolishness or deceitfulness may therein in any way have place. O Most Powerful and Ineffable God, Who madest Thy people pass dryshod through the Red Sea when they came up out of the Land of Egypt, grant unto me grace that I may be purified and regenerated from all my past sins by this*

---

74 See the Greater Key of Solomon book two pages 92-93.

Water, that so no uncleanness may appear upon me in Thy Presence. After this thou shalt entirely immerse thyself in the water, and thou shalt dry thyself with a towel of clean white linen, and then thou shalt put upon thy flesh the garments of pure white linen ..."[75]

Spirits and Experiments Concerning Water

I have looked through a few of the most popular grimoires to be able to list some of them here so you can see what they can help with in relation to water. Most of these spirits can help with many different things but for this essay we are concentrating on water so that is what I will tell you about for each spirit or experiment. For more detailed instructions you need to look in the texts I refer to as this is just intended to give a brief description of the water aspects and not complete operations.

Goetia

We can start by examining some spirits in the *Goetia*, the first book of the *Lemegeton*[76].

Focalor – This spirit has powers over wind and water and lakes to drown men and sink ships. The magician can order him not to harm anyone if he chooses to.

Vepar – His duty is to govern the seas and to guide ships loaded with arms, armor and so on. The magician can order him to make the ocean storm and appear as if it were full of ships.

Vine – This spirit's speciality when it comes to water is bringing on heavy storms.

Haagenti – This one specializes in transmutation and can turn water into wine and back again.

Crocell – This spirit can produce the sound of water. He can also heat water for you and find you baths. A great vacation spirit in other words!

---

75 From the Greater Key of Solomon book two page 86.
76 The Lemegeton is a collection of books where the Goetia is one of them. There are translations of the entire Lemegeton as well as only of the Goetia. Joseph Peterson's The Lesser Key of Solomon in the bibliography is actually the entire Lemegeton. The Lesser and Greater Key is actually something that De Laurance made up and called his pirated versions of The Key of Solomon and the Goetia that he stole straight of from S M L Mathers and is not a correct way of naming

Zagan – Another spirit that can turn water into wine and back again, but can also turn blood into wine.

7th book of Moses

In the *7th book of Moses* we have more spirits that can deal with water but to get their help we need to use different tables that you will see in the following examples:

"THE THIRD TABLE OF THE SPIRITS OF WATER
Conjuration
I call upon and command thee Chananya by God Tetragrammaton Eloh. I conjure Thee Yeschaijah by Alpha and Omega, and Thou art compelled through Adonai.

THE THIRD TABLE, FROM THE SIXTH AND SEVENTH BOOK OF MOSES BY EGYPTIAN PUBLISHING COMPANY PAGE 17.

The Third Table brings great fortune by water, and its spirits will amply supply the treasures of the deep."[77]

Here we also find the classical example of how Moses turned water in to blood:

"MOSES CHANGES WATER INTO BLOOD

---

them. See this article by David Rankine for more information http://grimoires.avalonia.co.uk/magic/greater_lesser_key.htm .
77 From the Sixth and Seventh Book of Moses by Egyptian Publishing Company page 17.

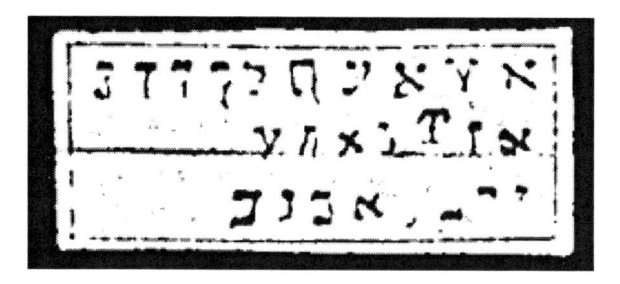

SEAL FROM THE SIXTH AND SEVENTH BOOK OF MOSES
BY EGYPTIAN PUBLISHING COMPANY PAGE 78.

The inscriptions on the seal are to be read as follows:
ABEN AGLA MANDEL SLOP SIEHAS MALIM HAJATH HAJADOSCH IJONEM,CEDAS EBREEL AMPHIA, DEMISRAEL MUELLE LEAGIJNS AMANIHA"[78]

Sword of Moses

In the *Sword of Moses* we can also find some very interesting passages on the use of water. The references to numbers 120 and 125 are explained in the original text.

"If thou walkest in vales or on the mountains and hast no water to drink, lift thine eyes to Heaven and say No.120, and a fountain of water will be opened unto thee."

"To walk upon the water without wetting the feet, take a leaden plate and write upon it No. 125 and place it in thy girdle, and then you can walk."

"To walk on the waters of the sea take the wooden helve of an axe, bore a hole through it, pass a red thread through it, and tie it on to thy heel, then repeat the words of the 'Sword,' and then you may go in and out in peace."[79]

The Book of Power

In Idries Shah's book *The Secret Lore of Magic* we find a translation of a manuscript that Shah calls *The Book of Power*. It contains a procedure to create the elixir of life or as it is also called the water of

---

[78] From the Sixth and Seventh Book of Moses by Egyptian Publishing Company page 78.
[79] From the Sword of Moses by Gaster Moses; Digital edition by Joseph H. Peterson.

life. The water of life is said to have the ability to extend life but has its drawbacks according to the text: apparently its users end up longing for death in the end.

The ritual involves first finding a stone that can only be found in the deserts of Africa and that is blue one side and red on the other. When you have found the stone you will have to do the following:

> "When you have found the stone, you must take it to a place far from the world of men, and there you must make for it a sheath, which is of copper and gold, and mount it therein, with the figure of a bird inscribed on it, and the words LI LI LI NA NA AN. Then you place it in water which you have brought from a running stream, and leave it there, alone and buried for the time during which seven moons wax and wane. And then, taking with you new clothes, and having bathed and eaten nothing, repair to that place. When you have the stone in your hand, say the words again and again, and place it on your heart. When this is finished, put off all your clothes, and make a fire from them. Then take up the new garments, and robe yourself. If they are green and white, it is better. Then take the water that has been with the stone, and it is the Water of Life. Half of it is to be placed in a small container, and this is to be stoppered and carried with you. The other half is to be drunk, when the sun comes up. Then you will live for the period for which you have prayed to be spared."[80]

Key of Solomon

From the *Key of Solomon* I would like to examine two of the pentacles[81] of the Moon.

The second pentacle of the Moon will protect you against all dangers at sea but has another useful feature if you are invoking spirits of the moon and they start to cause things like rain to irritate you: you can show them this pentacle and they will stop. The pentacle looks like this:

---

80 From Idries Shah's book The Secret Lore of Magic page 245-246.
81 A pentacle is the same as a talisman in this context.

THE SECOND PENTACLE OF THE MOON FROM THE KEY OF SOLOMON.

The third pentacle of the Moon also has the power to protect you from harm at sea but instead of protecting you against the spirits of the moon at evocations it protects you from harm at night wherever you are.

The next pentacle I would like to show you is the sixth pentacle of the Moon. If you put this pentacle under water it will start to rain and continue to do so until you take it out of the water again. This must be a great pentacle for farmers.

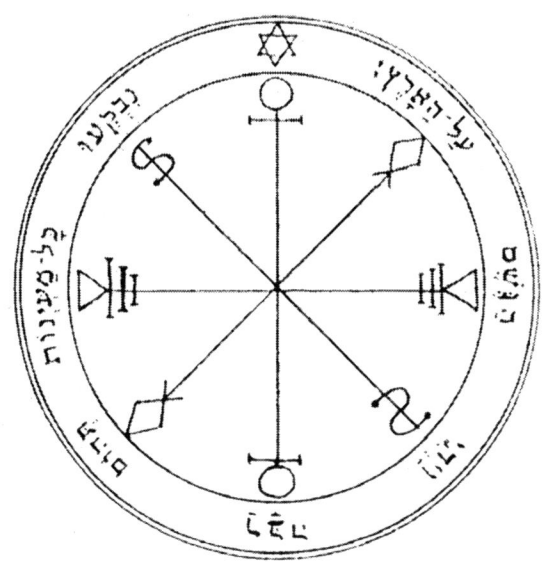

THE SIXTH PENTACLE OF THE MOON FROM THE KEY OF SOLOMON.

The Sacred Magic of Abramelin the Mage

In *The Sacred Magic of Abramelin the Mage* translated by S.L. McGregor Mathers there can be found magical squares that can do all kinds of wonderful things when drawn on parchment and activated through ritual. There are some that relate to water specifically that I will show you here.

If you own a mine that has been flooded with water, activating this seal will make the water withdraw from the mine:

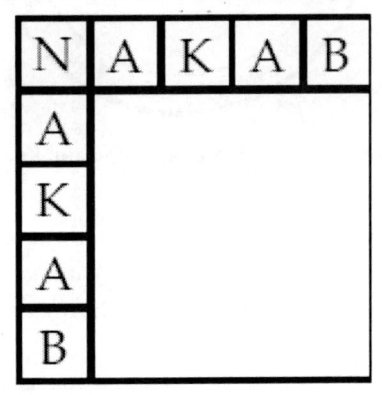

N	A	K	A	B
A				
K				
A				
B				

In case you need to swim for 24 hours without getting tired, activating this square will help you with that:

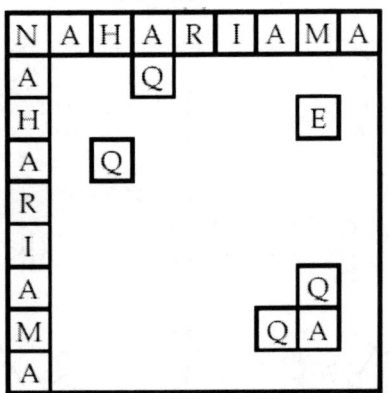

N	A	H	A	R	I	A	M	A
A			Q					
H							E	
A		Q						
R								
I								
A							Q	
M						Q	A	
A								

Perhaps you would then want to go under the water for two hours and look for treasure? Then you should activate this seal that let's you stay under water for two hours without the need to go up for air:

B	U	R	N	A	H	E	U
U	L	O	R	I	P	T	E
R	O	M	I	L	A	P	H
N	R	I	T	I	L	I	A
A	I	L	I	T	I	R	N
H	P	A	L	I	M	O	R
E	T	P	I	R	O	L	U
U	E	H	A	N	R	U	B

This next square lets you rest upon or walk on water for 24 hours:

M	A	I	A	M
A				
I				
A				
M				

This square when activated makes you see visions of fountains or clear water. Perhaps you need to make some holy water. Then this seal will come in handy.

N	E	S	I	K	E	R
E			Q			
S						
I	Q					
K						
E						
R						

107 | From a Drop of Water

Some last words

As we have seen in this essay water does play a rather central role to the traditional grimoire magician in form of consecration and preparations for the rituals. Holy water plays an important role as well as the baths. There are also a large number of magical operations that deal directly with water if you look for them. The following Bibliography shows all the books that I have used to get this information but they are just a small taster of the books I researched for relevant information.

Bibliography

Ch'ien, Kim; *The Grimoire of Pope Honorius III;* Trident Books; Seattle
Egyptian Publishing Company; *Sixth and Seventh Book of Moses*; 1996; Kessinger Publishing
Gaster Moses; *Sword of Moses*; 1988; Digital edition by Joseph H. Peterson; http://www.esotericarchives.com/solomon/sword.htm
Lisiewski, Joseph; *Ceremonial Magic & The power of Evocation*; 2008; The Original Falcon Press
Mathers, S L M; *The Key of Solomon the King*; 2009; Dover Publications
Mathers, S L M; *The Book of the Sacred Magic of Abramelin the Mage*, 1974; Dover Publications
Peterson, Joseph H. (ed); *The Lesser Key of Solomon*; 2001; Weiser Books; Maine
Rankine, David; d'Este, Sorita; *Practical Elemental Magic*; 2008; Avalonia Books
Rankine, David; Skinner, Stephen; Byron, Paul Harry; *A Collection of Magical Secrets & A Treatise of Mixed Cabalah*;2009; Avalonia Books
Rudy, Gretchen; *The Grand Grimoire*; Tridents Books; Seattle
Shah, Idries; *Secret Lore of Magic*; 1957; Frederick Muller LTD
Simon; *Papal Magic: Occult Practices Within the Catholic Church*; 2007; HarperCollins

NIMUE

THE ARCHETYPAL PRIESTESS

BY EMILY CARDING

"Whatever happened to my part?"
~The Lady of the Lake, Diva's Lament, Spamalot

Good question! Most of us are familiar with the image of the sacred sword Excalibur rising from the lake, but how much do we know about the figure beyond the shimmering samite-clad arm? On the other hand, we all know about the figure who leads Arthur to the lake, and for those who know less, there are reams of information that is easily available in books, the internet and within films and popular culture. Not many would argue with the fact that Merlin, in his various forms, is the archetypal magician. He transcends his existence as an historical and mythological figure, assimilating the various tales and conflicting descriptions of his character to become an amalgamated image with which most people, even those with no interest in magick, can readily identify.

To take this a step further, the power *behind* the stories and various versions of his character can be readily felt on a magickal level, and he clearly exists as a spiritual being in his own right with whom we can work and communicate. We don't tend to think of Merlin as an outright deity, and yet there are direct parallels and correspondences with various well-known deities from many cultures, most notably Hermes/Mercury, Odin and Thoth, so perhaps we can consider him to be an avatar of sorts. But however powerful and important the male polarity of magick as represented by Merlin as the archetypal magician is, where is the female polarity? Even in these Goddess-dominated times of magickal practice, Nimue, Lady of the Lake and the lover of Merlin, is still obscured and misunderstood.

> *"...Then, in one moment, she put forth the charm*
> *Of woven paces and of waving hands,*
> *And in the hollow oak he lay as dead,*
> *And lost to life and use and name and fame.*
>
> *Then crying "I have made his glory mine,"*
> *And shrieking out "O fool!" the harlot leapt*
> *Adown the forest, and the thicket closed*
> *Behind her, and the forest echoed "fool."..."*[82]

Here we see what remains the most persistent view of Nimue, (also known as Vivien, Vivienne, Niniane and so many other variants that names almost become irrelevant), as the evil enchantress who seduces and betrays the great and powerful Merlin with her feminine wiles. However this characterization is a relatively late development, growing out of an ignorance of the deeper mysteries that lie hidden within the myths. The above passage was written by Tennyson in the mid-nineteenth century, and its status as an inarguably great work of literature has had a huge influence over modern perceptions of Merlin's lover. However, if we look at another well-known source written four centuries earlier, the basic story is the same, but Nimue's character is rather more sympathetic:

> *"And always Merlin lay about the lady to have her maidenhood, and she was ever passing weary of him, and fain would have been delivered of him, for she was afeard of him because he was a devil's son..."*[83]

Malory drew on many different sources for his work, and that shows very clearly in the fact that his portrayal of Nimue, the Lady of the Lake, is highly inconsistent, ranging from entirely mortal and timid girl, to powerful Faery woman. There are however some nice hints hidden away in *Le Morte D'Arthur* that give us some clues as to her true power and importance. Most obvious of these is the fact that Nimue successfully and seamlessly takes over from Merlin as the protector and advisor of Arthur, who accepts her in this role without question. This is interesting, as Merlin was fully aware of the fact that Nimue was about to trap him and has informed Arthur of the fact and made his farewells.

---

82 Lord Alfred Tennyson, Merlin and Vivien, Idylls of the King.
83 Sir Thomas Malory, Le Morte D'Arthur, pp. 100

It is clearly a pre-arranged exit, and much more than a woman finding cunning means to be rid of her magical stalker! Another nice hint to her true nature can be found as the knight Sir Bagdemagus comes upon the stone beneath which Merlin is buried, and hears his voice emanating from the rock. However, the knight cannot lift it, and the voice of Merlin informs him that *"he might never be holpen but by her that put him there."* An obviously significant moment is the gifting of Excalibur to Arthur, where we can see that the power clearly lies with the Lady of the Lake, that Excalibur belongs to her, and will return to her in time. She is seen to walk on the water, and Merlin describes to Arthur how her land may be found under the surface of the Lake, clearly establishing her as being otherworldly in nature. Out of the whole text though, the most profound yet subtle insight can be found shortly after this event, when Merlin asks Arthur which he prefers, the sword or the scabbard. Arthur, (being a boy), makes the obvious choice and opts for the sword. *"You are more unwise, said Merlin, for the scabbard is worth ten of the swords..."*

For those of us who like our esoteric symbolism, does this not imply that the real power lies with the receptive female?

Going back another three centuries we find another very well-known source, that of the works of Geoffrey of Monmouth. In his *History of the Kings of Britain*, the first known work to bring the stories of Arthur and Merlin together, there is no mention of Nimue or Merlin's fate. However if we look at his later work, *The Life of Merlin*, or *Vita Merlini* we are presented with several very interesting women who could be seen as aspects of a female polarity for Merlin. In her fascinating *Ladies of the Lake*, one of the only books that seems to focus on the powerful women of Arthurian myth, Caitlin Matthews observes the links between the figures of Nimue and Merlin's twin sister Ganeida, who also has powers of prophecy. Ganeida is a powerful woman in her own right, being the consort of King Rodarch, and it is she who enables Merlin's retreat from the world, creating for him a wonderful starry observatory where she visits him often. Interestingly Merlin also has a wife, Guendolena, but the two characters seem so interchangeable that it is reasonable to theorise that they may be derived from an original sister/lover figure that was separated into two aspects to be more sociably acceptable. Another possibility is that together with Morgen, who appears in this text as the ruler of the Otherworld, or land of Faery, they are an echo of an older triple-goddess figure. This darker female figure reappears in later texts as Arthur's ambiguous half-sister, Morgan Le Fay, through whose challenges Arthur and his knights are able to truly test their limits and prove themselves, making her an equally important initiator. It is assumed that Geoffrey of Monmouth was drawing on much earlier sources for his inspiration that have now been lost to us. He certainly encapsulates many elements of the Welsh historical figure of Myrddin Wylt, who also had a twin sister of similar name, Gwendydd, and gains powers of prophecy after losing his mind and running mad in the forest.

We could sit for days, weeks and months looking at the literary sources, of which there are many, and wondering about the origins and truth of the characters within, but one source that is instantly accessible is that of spiritual inspiration, intuition and the reality of the Otherworld. It has been my lifelong feeling that there is much more to Nimue than the surface tale of love and betrayal, more even than her role as initiator of kings, although this is clearly a significant aspect. The symbolism of the sword rising from the lake is potent indeed, as is the idea of the Lady of the Lake as a representative of the land itself, with the power to grant sovereignty- but what does it mean on its deepest level?

> "*King Arthur: I am your king!*
> *Woman: Well I didn't vote for you.*
> *King Arthur: You don't vote for kings.*
> *Woman: Well how'd you become king then?*
> *King Arthur: The Lady of the Lake, her arm clad in the purest shimmering samite held aloft Excalibur from the bosom of the water, signifying by divine providence that I, Arthur, was to carry Excalibur. THAT is why I am your king.*
> *Dennis: [interrupting] Listen, strange women lyin' in ponds distributin' swords is no basis for a system of government."*
> ~ *Monty Python and the Holy Grail*

Considering the way governments are being run at the moment, we could do a lot worse than return to this system. As we have already established, the Lady of the Lake is quite clearly a Faery woman, or at the very least a priestess representative of the Otherworldly realm. The sword, symbol of truth and rightful authority, rises through the waters from the land of Faery, the realm hidden from the reach of ordinary mortals in the hollow places beneath the ground. The power of the sword *belongs* to the Lady of the Lake, and hence to Faery, and is only wielded for a time by mortal man, to be returned to whence it came at the time of his passing. Just as the elemental symbol for water represents the female magickal polarity, so water itself here represents the ability of the archetypal priestess to act as a veil between worlds, and to bring wisdom and power through from one realm into another. In this case, the lake acts as the medium through which an object of power can physically travel from one realm to another, and the Lady of the Lake is the consciousness that controls the process and physically represents the authority of the Otherworld. It is no accident or surprise that the truth behind this female power has been systematically wiped out or concealed over the years of male-dominated Christian rule, but it is a shame that even some supposedly magical people still hold the manufactured perception of Nimue as being treacherous and deceitful. I have even seen one woman insist that another should not be admitted to a group working with Merlin because her chosen magickal name was Nimue!

However, those wise enough to see beyond the surface to the deeper truths have brought out some real gems. One example is a rather wonderful sex magick ritual called *The Ritual of the Hawthorn Tower* in a book called *The Tree of Ecstasy* by the esoteric author and teacher, Dolores Ashcroft-Nowicki. The book is an exploration of the Tree of Life and the rebalancing of power between male and female, and contains a series of exacting preparations and rituals that correspond to each sephiroth. *The Ritual of the Hawthorn Tower* corresponds to the sphere of Netzach and uses the polarity of Merlin and Nimue as the roles for the priest and priestess. The author explains that the intention of the ritual is *"...for Merlin to summon the enchantress and persuade her to open the ancient door between the worlds. It is she that holds the key that will release him from the world of men... In human terms the intention is for the woman to open the door of intuition to man."*[84]

This sounds very much like what we would expect from an archetypal priestess to match our magician. Interestingly she also writes about Merlin's half-human nature making him an appropriate archetype for the sphere of Netzach, suggesting that his supposedly 'demonic' father was in fact of Faery origin. This is not anything particularly new, as it is well established in most versions of the myth

---

84 Dolores Ashcroft-Nowicki, The Tree of Ecstasy, pp. 145

that Merlin is born of a human mother and non-human father, who is described as being either a demon, an angel, a faery, or the devil himself, but it does raise the interesting question as to the truth of Merlin's nature, and hence, (if they are a true polarity), that of his partner, Nimue.

Another treasure can be found in an all too brief essay by the esotericist Gareth Knight in an anthology called *The Book of Merlin*, edited by R.J. Stewart. In this essay, entitled *Merlin and Nimue*, he converses with a hawthorn tree which tells him its own version of events, in which the motivations of Nimue are purely love for Merlin and doing what must be done for the sake of the future redemption of the land. When asked what will become of the people of Earth without the guidance of Merlin, the tree replies, *"When Nimue, the earth maiden has learned all the star lore of Merlin, and Merlin has learned the earth lore of Nimue, then the two will go hand in hand in cosmic marriage to the stars, taking the children of earth with them."* This single sentence contains within it some very interesting thoughts for the open mind to ponder. Could it be referring to the unity of Nimue and Merlin as being symbolic of a new magickal system, one that unites the path of ceremonial magick with more earthy and intuitive shamanic, traditional nature-based practices? At the same time it makes me think back to my essay, *The Salvation of the Sidhe* written for another Avalonia anthology, *Both Sides of Heaven*, in which I explored the connections between the Faery race and the fallen angels. A key point that arose was the idea that the Sidhe, being cast out into the hollow places of the earth, were awaiting the time when they would achieve 'salvation' and return to their true home and rightful place. I compared this idea with the symbolism of the Tarot card Judgement and the idea of the spiritual evolution of the human race, with the aid and cooperation of their Faery cousins. Exploring the theme of fallen angels further, we return to the subject of Merlin's parentage and Nimue's faery nature.

As already mentioned, Merlin's conception is the result of a union between a mortal woman and a supernatural father of varied description, most commonly a demon. Could this not have been, in fact, a fallen angel? In his work, *The Book of Fallen Angels*, Michael Howard discusses the teachings of Madeline Montalban and the premise that *"the fallen archangel is destined to be reborn time and time again in human form as a saviour and take upon himself the pain, sorrows and suffering of humankind"*, and goes on to describe the various possible avatars of Lucifer, including Jesus Christ. He quotes a passage from *The Book of Lumiel* in which Lumiel/Lucifer states that he *"...was the scapegoat, to be driven into the wilderness suffering shame and ignorance life after life"*. Does this not fit well with the life of Merlin, who found his gift of wisdom and prophecy after running wild in the forest? Is his departure from the world not because of the suffering of mankind that he has taken onto himself? It might also be worth mentioning that both Lucifer and Merlin have a connection to apple trees, in one case the tree of knowledge, in the other we see one of the best known poems attributed to the historical Merlin himself, *'Afallennau'*, from the *Black Book of Carmarthen*, in which he sings the praises of the apple tree, (and also mentions his sister, Gwendydd). Returning to the *Vita Merlini*, there is also description of *'poisoned apples'* which cause men to lose their minds. R.J. Stewart links this directly with the fruit of the Tree of Life, which in Faery tradition grows between the rivers of tears and blood in the underworld.

Perhaps we can see Merlin as an avatar of Lucifer, fathered by the fallen angel himself? This becomes particularly interesting when we return to Nimue and her connections. Several authors have noted the prose *Merlin*, a French text that predates Malory as a source for uncovering Nimue's true nature. This text emphasizes the importance of Nimue's father and his dedication to the lunar Goddess of the hunt, Diana. In her book *Ladies of the Lake*, Caitlin Matthews even goes as far to say that *"...it is possible, initially, to see that Diana, the Goddess...may at one time have been the actual mother of Nimue"*,[85] and goes on to demonstrate the many connections with this Goddess and the Lady of the Lake. Returning to Michael Howard's *Book of Fallen Angels*, he discusses various sources which connect Lucifer and Diana as a male/female polarity, including Leland's *Aradia: Gospel of the Witches*, and also demonstrates the connections in Roman myth between Diana and Hecate, returning to the triple goddess motif. (If this is a valid connection, which it does indeed seem to be, then Hecate's role as key-bearer fits well with the role of Nimue as keeper of the doors between worlds. Also there is an echo of the pairing of Hecate with Hermes, one of the prime deities associated with Merlin.) So this gives a fresh insight into the nature of Merlin and Nimue, as avatars and/or offspring of a divine polarity on a higher vibration. The other element

---

85 Caitlin Matthews, Ladies of the Lake, pp.111

that binds Merlin/Nimue together with Lucifer/Diana as a pairing is, of course, the Grail myth.

There are almost as many visions and interpretations of the myth of the Grail as there are people to seek them. One of the more established myths is that of the Grail as the emerald which fell from Lucifer's crown in The Fall. This in itself is a mine of symbolism and knowledge that is best discussed at more length elsewhere. Merlin, through his involvement in the Arthurian mythos, is also intrinsically connected to the search for the Grail. In truth, perhaps each of us seeks our own individual Grail, the truth of the self. This is one of the main principles behind the Merlin's Wisdom work which is facilitated by my husband Julian Clark, John Parker and Wil Kinghan. I mention this because of a personal experience of Julian's that I would like to discuss, which happened during a Merlin working. An inhumanly tall figure in a black and silver hooded robe of an unusual otherworldly energy appeared to them, who, when asked to reveal himself declared that they were not yet ready to look upon his true appearance. However, the feeling was that of the brilliance of a star, veiled by darkness...

Meanwhile, back in the essay I'm *supposed* to be writing, how does this add to the significance of Nimue and the Lady of the Lake as Merlin's female counterpart? If Merlin's power does indeed come from the realm of stars as brought to us by the fallen angel, then Nimue's comes from the inner earth and projects outwards, just as Excalibur is brought forth from the lake. As Merlin can be seen as the archetypal Magician of the Tarot, Nimue is without doubt his High Priestess, guardian of the veil that hides the true source of magick. As a priestess, is she in service to any particular deity? Gareth Knight compares her stealing of Merlin's secrets to Isis discovering Ra's secret name and hence becoming mistress of magick. However, it is my feeling that she is a priestess of the element of water itself, and that the Lady of the Lake as we know her now is actually a reflection or echo of an ancient tradition of cooperation with the Faery realm. Hers is the power of the underworld waters of regeneration and healing, and the initiation of the cauldron. From the waters, the source of birth, life and female power, she brings forth that which may be wielded for a short time by the male. Through working with the energy of Nimue we can restore healing to the land, and build new bridges with the Faery realm. In an idealistic way we can hope that we may find a leader whom the Lady of the Lake will deem worthy, and the sword will rise once more. However, the time of blindly following a single leader is past, and it is now time for each of us to take on the responsibility ourselves, to bear the sword, be one with the land and rulers of our own realities.

Obviously I have touched on many areas here, some of which lead off like myriad branches in their own directions and could probably fill a book of their own if given the time and space. However, the main point is this: the joining together of these polarities of above and below in balance as represented by Merlin and Nimue in her rightful place offer the opportunity to unlock inner potential, knowledge and awakening. In conclusion, I would like to offer you my own version of their tale, in the form of *'Nimue's Song'*...

Nimue's Song: A Lost Tale by Emily Carding

I have been silent for far too long,
The truth must be told so hear my song,
Will you hear the words of a heart that sighs,
Or cling to an old monk's dusty lies?

Hear me now and my tale of woe,
A tale of love that spirits know,
A tale of above, a tale of below,
A tale of here and now and long ago...

The moonlit Huntress' daughter, I,
Came to you through a watery sky,
You knew my face,
You spoke my name,
And in that place we lit a flame.

Star-seed children, kindred souls,
Torn asunder, together we're whole,
At once we knew,
In morning dew,
What it meant to be as one

The magic grew strong as I lay in your arms,
And it's true when they say,
That you taught me your charms,
You showed me the Stars,
But I showed you the Moon,
Together we danced a writhing Beltane tune!

We were the land, the land was us,
We opened our hearts to sacred trust,
We loved and the blessed balance kept,
We fought and the sky with thunder wept

I am the keeper of the door,
But you unlock my evermore,
Come sing of love and I'll set you free,
Under ancient Hawthorn Tree

Then came all the wars of mortal men,
And chaos ruled the ways again,
We studied their hearts, their loves, their fears,
We watched and waited for all those years

In deep Annwn was born a sword,
From Fire and Ice and Stone was't forged,
It waited silent in my guard,
To heal the shattered throne

So you brought forth a shining soul,
To bear the sword and make the land whole,
But light will always darkness bring,
And shadows lay in the fate of this king

And though you knew, his end you saw,
You could not break the sacred law,
Heavy it lay upon your heart,
And we danced in glade no more

"So little time", I wept to know,
"But the Land and I both need you so!"
You asked to die with a pleading face,
And your life began to fade

But I could never, never let that be,
And I wept as I took you to our Hawthorn tree,
Within the land of moonless sky,
Your voice became a whispered cry...

"The stars are cold without you love,
I need to touch and hold you love,
Need your heart to make me whole,
Need your love to set me free..."

Merlin, love, my soul's true fire,
I never betrayed you, I am no liar!
I hold you still within my heart,
Always together, forever apart

I am the keeper of the door,
I am the holder of the key,
I'll sing your song of Nevermore,
Under ancient Hawthorn tree

But when the sword does rise again,
And when, at last, the land's reborn,
Your heart will beat with mine again,
And we will love,
And we will love,
And we will dance once more...

Bibliography

Matthews, Caitlin and John, *Ladies of the Lake*, 1992, Thorsons, London, UK
Howard, Michael, *The Book of Fallen Angels*, 2004, Capall Bann, Somerset, UK
D'Este, Sorita (ed), *Both Sides of Heaven*, 2009, Avalonia, London, UK
Stewart, R.J. (ed), *The Book of Merlin*, 1987, Blandford Press, Dorset, UK
Stewart, R.J., *The Mystic Life of Merlin*, 1986, Routledge and Kegan Paul Ltd., London, UK
Malory, Sir Thomas, *Le Morte D'Arthur*, 2000, Cassell and Co, London, UK
Tennyson, Lord Arthur, *Idylls of the King*
Ashcroft-Nowicki, Dolores, The Tree of Ecstasy, 1991, The Aquarian Press, London, UK

QUENCHING THE THIRST, DRINKING THE SPIRIT

WATER AND WATER GUARDIANS IN ROOT MAGICK

BY JOHN CANARD

When I was first asked to write for this unique anthology I wasn't sure whether to accept the invitation. One of the things about root magick is that it is not a hard and fast system, full of clear definitions and absolute rules and methodologies. Rather, it is a philosophy around which practices coalesce, like the pearl which bejewels a grain of sand inside an oyster. Whilst many practices will inevitably be found in common amongst root magicians, an equal or greater number may be more localised to particular lines or locations. Nevertheless, with water playing such a key role in root magick, I felt I had to take the opportunity to present my personal view on the magic of water.

Water is not just water. The unique nature of water is emphasised by its ability to carry essences within itself. Water is the menstruum of life, and as such plays a key role in root magick, from morning dew to Donar water to the flowing water of streams and springs. The beings associated with water also have their roles to play, and are far too often ignored considering their significance in the magick of transformation and growth. As with many other magickal matters, timing is extremely relevant in dealing with water, both for gathering and for using it. I have discussed the blessing of water elsewhere,[86] and here will focus rather on the types of water and their uses.

The morning dew, kissed by the first rays of the sun, has always been seen as magickal. What is often ignored however is the equally liminal evening dew, formed as the sun sets. Both forms of dew may be gathered and used for rites. The morning dew is particularly appropriate for the salt and water used to purify a space, or for blessing magickal items. The evening dew can be used to complete cycles, and is

---

86 Defences Against the Witches' Craft, Canard, 2008.

ideal for blessing plants when the harvest is gathered, for their period of repose.

Traditionally dew was gathered on Beltane morning, but it can be gathered at any time of the year for use, though I prefer Beltane and St John's Day (24th June). The folk tradition of Beltane dew being rubbed on maidens' faces to preserve beauty emphasises the quality of dew as a regenerative medium, which promotes fertility, both physically and mentally. Dew is also associated with resurrection, and may be used as an offering to ancestors when performing work with your forefathers and foremothers, or other spirits of the dead. The best way of gathering dew is a dew pond, however this is outside the realms of practicality for most people, who do not have the outdoor space, and so clean non-porous ceramic bowls are a simple way to collect uncontaminated dew. When you first pick up your container of dew, hold it up to the heavens and proclaim:

> "Waters of heaven, you carry the blessings of the sun and sky, sanctus, sanctus, sanctus."

Another type of magickal water I frequently use is 'Donar water', so called after the Germanic thunder god, due to it being water gathered during a thunderstorm. From a magickal perspective this water is very powerful, as it has a higher than normal electrical charge attached to it. When the lightning strikes and the thunder booms, then you should be putting bowls out in the garden to collect the Donar water (also sometimes called invigorated water). I particularly use Donar water for spells and rites that require a strong element of growth. It may also be used for encouraging plants to grow, particularly if you are trying to cultivate herbs which are trickier to work with, like mandrake, ginger or galangal.

Of course we also produce our own forms of water in saliva, tears, and sweat. It used to be common practice to spit on your hand before shaking hands to seal a deal. Obviously this reflected the view that saliva is literally flavoured with the words of power of the magician (or non-magician), and is a very powerful substance. This is why many curses include spitting at a person or in their direction. Spit, like tears, is personally empowered water from within, and as such can carry a very strong charge to heal or harm. Putting a drop of your spit onto a seed before planting it, after speaking a blessing, is a good way to promote growth, and likewise when harvesting wild plants saliva can be used as an alternative to blood as an offering to the spirit of the plant, particularly if empowered with a suitable spoken charm first.

An interesting old practice from my homelands of the Cambridgeshire fens was to spit on a piece of old iron and throw it away for good luck. If you ever found the piece of iron again you had to repeat the ritual. The magickal power of saliva combined with that of iron was obviously considered a strong charm, as this was a popular practice.

Moving on to water from within the earth, any root magician will always know where the local springs and wells are: it is one of those essential pieces of local lore you have to find out at the beginning of your apprenticeship. Springs and wells bring water from within the earth to the surface for our use, and have always been seen as sacred. Healing wells and springs formed the focus for many Celtic healing deities, and for good reason. The chthonic power infused into such water makes it good for all manners of root magick. Such water should always be gathered in ceramic or glass vessels (not plastic or metal!) to avoid any dispersal of the energy in the water.

If you grow your own herbs for magickal use, then it is worth making the effort to visit your nearest spring or well to gather water for nurturing them. The ideal time to gather water from a spring is Epiphany, which used to be known as the feast day for wells. Obviously you would gather water at regular intervals so it does not stand for too long without being used. A charm for protection from fairies and witches is to walk three times sunwise round a sacred well or spring, drink from the water, and then throw a pin in. This is a great example of sympathetic magick, with the link being made between the person and the well, and then the protective iron thrown into the well to have its power magnified and returned to the person. Of course you would ask the guardian of the place first, before throwing in any sort of offering, no matter how well-meaning it might be!

Well and spring guardians may come from a number of sources. They may be old goddesses, undines, genius loci, fortified human souls, or even thought forms. What is significant is that they are usually viewed as women, and are often seen as being dressed in blue and white. These are also the Marian colours associated with the Virgin Mary, and the Egyptian goddess Isis previously to that. However the association of blue with water is ancient, and the white of purity, also representing the foam on moving water, is appropriate for such guardians. Many people today seem to ignore such watery guardians, and yet considering the ability of water to carry an emotional or magickal charge, this seems either blasé or stupid. On approaching any well or spring the obvious thing to do is to present an attitude of respect. Offerings if made should be appropriate – it is not appropriate to put things into the water source, be they crystals, other water or liquid, or whatever. Likewise leaving candle stubs at sites, or tying plastic items to trees because there are cloth strips already present are further demonstrations of the sort of thoughtlessness that goes on. Some sites have a tradition of casting pins or coins into them as offerings, which is clearly derived from the old practice of votive offerings. Votive offerings are best made at places with such a history, hence the tradition of wishing wells!

The appropriate offerings you can make are twofold – either of physical work clearing away any rubbish you find in the vicinity, or energetically by giving a gift of energy to the guardian. In such an instance you could offer a prayer of thanks to the guardian and burn a suitable dried herb you have collected previously, like watercress or lesser duckweed, so the energy of your prayer is carried on the smoke into the air where it can be absorbed by the guardian in its own manner. Of course you would remove your charcoal and any burnt remnants with you, rather than just dumping them on a piece of earth, or worse into the water!

There are also many local water spirits who have become viewed as malicious, who may have originally been seen as river guardians. These are characters such as the Grindylow, Jenny Greenteeth, Nelly Long-Arms and Peg Powler.

Today gem elixirs have become very popular, but the idea of blessing gems in holy water from wells is not new, as can be seen in the following blessing. This blessing occurs around Britain, being found in versions with the Keppoch charm-stone in Scotland, in Wales and in Somerset. The version below which I heard in Somerset seems to be a hybrid of the Scottish and Welsh charms.

> *O Thou stone of Might and Right*
> *Let me dip thee in the water,*
> *In water of pure spring or wave,*
> *Which pure was kept by Bridget.*
> *In the name of the Apostles twelve,*

> *In the name of Mary, virgin of virtues,*
> *And in the name of Michael, Gabriel, Raphael*
> *And all the shining angels.*
> *A blessing on the gem,*
> *A blessing on the water,*
> *And a healing of all bodily ailments*
> *To man and beast alike!*

A completely different technique that I have not seen used anywhere except in root magick is that of immersion prayer. This is an old technique from Anglo-Saxon times still used today, where you pray whilst immersed in water up to your neck. Many early saints followed this practice, in pools, rivers and the sea, usually reciting from the book of Psalms. Such immersion with prayer was considered a very powerful healing technique when performed in the sea, and one that has been used through into recent times. It should be done as the tide goes out, taking away ailments with it. Appropriate verses from Psalms should be sought first, and committed to memory. If however you wish to gain something rather than have something taken away, you should pray immersed whilst the tide comes in. Ideally you should time your prayer so it ends on the ninth wave going past you each time, as the ninth wave is traditionally the most powerful and beneficial.

So, from the first drop of dew to the last wave, the power of water nourishes our roots, whether we are magicians, plants or anything in-between!

Bibliography

Bonser, Wilfrid; *Praying in Water*; 1937, in *Folklore* 48.4:385-88
Canard, John; *Defences Against the Witches' Craft*; 2008; Avalonia; London
----------; unpublished correspondence with Hilda Starling, 1975-present
Stewart, Rev. Alexander; *Proceedings of the Society of Antiquaries of Scotland*; 1890
Trevelyan, Marie; *Folk-lore and Folk-stories of Wales*; 1909

THE QUEEN OF THE OCEANS

THE AFRO-BRAZILIAN GODDESS YEMANYÁ AND SEA MAGIC

BY ANDREA SALGADO REYES

Africa and water are closely allied with the image of drought, certainly in the past century, and what has elapsed of this one doesn't seem to promise any improvement. That is one type of power: the devastation caused by the lack of an element. Yet its opposite also still exists.

In the early '80s my mother Myriam and I flew over the Ocean to reach the mighty Zambezi River and exclaimed over its vastness. One of the ferrymen told me that it used to be much wider and deeper, that in his grandfather's time it was much more dangerous to cross. I watched what seemed to be huge logs floating on its surface like twigs and could imagine nothing larger, anywhere. It seemed so calm, peaceful, meandering. Until a *'log'* opened its mouth and I realized we were surrounded by crocodiles hoping for a feed. It is a river full of life and death. Death which thrives on life; life which thrives on death. A circle sustained and nourished by the water.

It may seem strange to begin an essay on sea magic by writing of a river yet of course their cycles are entirely allied. It is impossible to separate one from the other for both are states of water as an element. To speak of the sea and of the great rivers which feed it in Africa is to speak of life in full force and enormous range. In African magic water is very important and there are many types of water: Firstly, sweet water and salt water; shallow water and deep waters; fast-flowing and stagnant; water which brings wealth and water which brings disease; water which brings love and water which drowns love and sweeps it away; water for purification of the body, of places and objects; water which gives health by drinking or bathing.

Even one body of water has many layers and uses: the sea by day; the sea by night; the sea at first light; the sea at dusk. Deep sea, where one has to row out to leave offerings to the beings of the dark; and the space between there and the shore, in which the waves ride high with much foam. Offerings given to the depths are different to offerings made to float out to sea and different again from offerings made at the shore itself, for the sea to take if it will, at high tide or by miraculously high wave. Sympathetic magic some, quite obviously, like sea shells. Some seemingly opposed, like bonfires or dozens of candles which can only be put out by the sea water, offerings to Yemanyá. What can the sea want with fire?

Sweet water and its more usual manifestations: rivers, streams, waterfalls; lakes, ponds and pools; wells and other inner earth water like that found inside caves or coming from earth or rock fissures. Each with their own beings and guardians which can act for or against humans, depending on their nature and how they are approached. Rain water, fog, mist and dew which can all be gathered for use or otherwise manipulated for magical purposes. All eventually completing and renewing their cycles in the oceans, through evaporation, rain and rivers.

The most potent fact to remember is that in African magic there is one uniting concept for water: water is alive. It is crammed full of life and energy which can be used mundanely and magically.

2nd February, the feast day of Yemanyá, She Whose Children Are Fish. Beaches in Brazil, Uruguay and Argentina fill with the women and men of the diaspora religions of the *Orixás*: *Candomblé, Umbanda, Palo Mayombe* and *Santería*. Women of all ages dressed in wide white skirts and white blouses, bosoms laden with shell and glass necklaces, with pearls and crystal beads: barefoot, they enter the sea to the waist, taking with them baskets of offerings, bouquets of white roses, flower garlands, gold jewellery, silver-backed mirrors, and fine combs. They sing Her praises while on the beach African drums sound out the particular beats that call Her. On the beach hundreds of white and blue candles flicker and the shape which is Her sacred symbol is drawn on the sands and laid out with cowrie shells. Vessels of all kinds set sail for the open seas, bearing golden jewellery, perfume to cast upon the waters, fine new clothing in Her colours, her favourite food and many requests written on paper which her devotees believe she will grant once they are delivered into her kingdom.

Yemanyá in her *Okuti* aspect is the Queen of Witches, owner of the magic of the oceans and all their deep and dark secrets. To all, She is mother to the *Orixás* and to humankind; and her children are numberless. All the inhabitants of the sea belong to her, the riches of the ship wrecks, the corpses, the buried towns and villages in Her salty domain, the spirits and countless entities of the oceans obey Her as their Queen. A vast realm which is ever changing and rich, filled with Her peace and also with Her anger. The first cauldron of life from which we all emerge. The *Orixá* of journeys, all must ask Her permission to cross the seas safely, even in airplanes, and pay Her a tribute for having arrived at their destination.

A devotee may seek the fulfilment of a simple wish: work or health or an errant husband to be returned home. She may also be invoked, as the Great Mother, to protect a difficult birth or to safeguard a wayward child or one for whom there have been bad omens. All that is required is a simple altar at home or by the sea, dressed in Her colours and the request must be accompanied by the traditional offerings. She is well known for being very approachable and a kind mother to Her devotees. However, if spurned or insulted, She has a vengeful and cruel aspect, with a very long memory. Her strength and determination are unbreakable.

Magic wielded by a *mae de santo* and her trainees is a much more convoluted affair than the devotee level. Altars are elaborate and permanent, always being added to with offerings and gifts for the deity. Ritual clothing is required both for priestesses, to dress the cult statues and to dress those who are taken by possession during rituals.

In serving the *Orixás*, their priests and priestesses take on many of their attributes – if they were not born with them, that is - and Yemanyá´s daughters are said to be tall, swaying, and voluptuous and of motherly aspect in later years. They are expected to be scrupulously clean and sweet smelling, always dressed in white and blue, in seven-layered skirts representing the seven seas.

Their work is varied. They are reputed to be excellent healers and are in much demand to foretell the future with the shells, purify spaces, lift curses, and remove hexes. Entering the priesthood, becoming a *mae de santo*, requires much self-discipline and the willingness to work within a very hierarchical structure. A properly run *terreiro* (ritual enclosure and temple) has special rooms to keep the deity's belongings, kitchens to prepare food for festivities and offerings, many porcelain and clay vessels in which objects of power and spellwork are kept, as well as all the ingredients which might be required for making them.

Music is also an important aspect of rites, the sacred drums and rattles. The dances in Her rites are representations of the movement of the waters of the sea, wide sweeps of skirt and undulating long hair, limbs loose and fluid, now slow and languorous, now fast and flowing like choppy waters. Many shell necklaces and belts are worn.

The types of magic which are done in Yemanyá's name are manifold.

Prosperity is the domain of Yemanyá – which She shares with Oxún, Goddess of rivers and sweet waters- and Her devotees seek Her help to achieve better employment, to win competitions and lotteries, to buy a home. In exchange they offer her sumptuous gifts when the working shows results.

Yemanyá is reputed to aid women who suffer because of the abuses of men and will swiftly punish evil-doers. Methods for this are numerous, including whipping effigies of the men concerned, using chillies and other preparations in spells to cause painful reactions in genitalia of sexual abusers, binding puppets with steel chains representing the will of the Goddess.

Being the mother of all, Her help is sought by women having difficulties conceiving and also in finding a suitable partner with whom to form a family. Romance is usually the realm of Oxún but Yemanya may also grant such petitions if the purpose is to set up a home and have children, rather than a romance by itself.

She is a fierce defender of Her priestesses, to whom She grants beauty, wisdom, magical power and strength which is unbreakable. They are also granted quiet authority and a regal manner. No one may attempt to harm Her chosen, not even with magic from other *Orixás*, as She is senior to them all, being the mother of fifteen *Orixás*, one of them being Ossaín the magician and another Ogún the warrior, also in some legends one of her husbands. Her magick is not restricted to the sea, but that being Her realm, it is Her great strength.

Yemanyá also commands the hosts of beings which belong to her father Olokun, who dwells in the depths of the sea. Among the sea beings who serve Her are the sirens and mermaids, alluring creatures reputed to drive insane with desire those who find them, thus punishing, for instance, men who break vows of fidelity and undying love to their lovers. In the depths of the sea are where She keeps her most secret magic and where Her priestesses may seek magical creatures to avenge wrongs and to defend themselves from attacks. The source of primordial magic is also there, in vast quantities. The very first primordial beings still reside there, huge creatures of similar nature to the leviathan; once called upon, only blood tributes may still them once again and make them return to their kingdoms. To call upon them in Yemanyá's name without just cause is to earn the wrath of the Goddess whatever the rank or initiation of the summoner.

Closer to the surface, there are gentler creatures which may be called upon to aid divination and to open paths to visit the deeper realms; kind guides and playful companions, who by their very enchanting nature may turn dangerous as the joy their presence brings becomes addictive. A deeper study of the types of elemental beings which inhabit different seas; and of local folklore- as well as beings already known to *Orixá* initiates- reap high dividends when looking for particular effects and results.

Rewarding avenues to explore in magic with Yemanyá are the symbols which represent Her and their use in making amulets and talismans, for instance carved onto sea shells or onto turquoise. Together with offerings by the sea and prayers immersed in the sea itself while holding the amulet in the waves to request protection, making an amulet is simple and very effective. One calls upon Yemanyá in her mother aspect to grant protection.

As Yemanyá is the loving mother, so can she be the tempestuous sea, bringing turmoil and fear. During such times, it is recommended that She be appeased with offerings at the water's edge. Her ritual foods, candles in Her colours and the gifts already described cast into the waters can bring calm and plenty again, even when one has transgressed the rules of the invisible realms, polluted them or offended by neglect or unjust acts.

A talisman for wealth must be paid for. One very successful ritual which I did about a decade ago entailed purchasing two handfuls of sea pearls and a handful of small nuggets of turquoise. Coupled with plentiful white roses and a bottle of champagne, they made a suitable gift for my request: a piece of land within sight of the sea on which to develop a pagan community. Duly purified and dressed in a white garment, I set up an altar and greeted Yemanyá. I entered the sea shortly after dawn during a full moon. I poured the champagne into the water near the shore, then swam a little further out, made my request and scattered the area with the pearls and turquoise.

A year later, I set out with two relatives to find a place to live near the coast, in that country. We began some 250 kilometres further up the coast. It was to be a joint decision which place we chose. When we drove into that particular bay, having seen several very beautiful beaches, they both immediately said we had arrived at an excellent place. They didn´t know of the ritual I had done.

We found our piece of land 3 kilometres away, within two days, and the deal made with the owners was excellent, within our modest budget, in an area with much more expensive land all around which we could not have afforded. It continues to be an excellent place for us and for many others who visit us for neo-pagan rites. I hold an annual ceremony on that beach in honour of Yemanyá, to thank Her for Her aid.

Mayans, Maize and Much-Needed Rain

By Rachel Donaldson

To the ancient Mayan farmer nothing was more precious to him than his maize field. It was his life blood and the farmer identified with his maize as a living animate object – it had a soul. Like the farmer, the maize had a fragile existence and was beset by a number of perils including disease, animals and fire. However, what maize needed most of all to survive was rain. Rain was the creator that made the maize grain grow but it could also be its destructor if there were too much rain. Maize and its relationship with the rain formed one basis of the dualistic Mayan religion which was the concept of cyclic creation and destruction. Both maize and rain had divine status.

The rain gods had a pivotal role to play in the discovery of maize. The legend says that maize was stored under a vast mountain and was first discovered by a great army of marching ants. The ants were small enough to creep into a small hole in the mountain and take the maize out, grain by grain, into the world. While the ants were absorbed in this activity they were spotted by a fox whose curiosity led him to eat one of the maize grains. Soon the tale of the ant's grains spread throughout the animal kingdom and finally to man. Man appealed to the rain gods to help them access the vast store of maize grain still under the mountain. Three of the rain gods tried to break open the mountain with their thunder bolts but failed in their attempt. Finally, the fourth and oldest rain god, who had not been that interested in the task up to now, consented to try. He asked the woodpecker to peck away at the mountain and find the weakest spot, once found the rain god told the woodpecker to hide while he used all his might to tear asunder the mountain. After several attempts one massive thunderbolt did the trick and the mountain was torn open. Unfortunately, the woodpecker decided to stick his head out just at that moment and was struck in the head by a large piece of rock causing him to bleed, after that the woodpecker was destined to have a red head. So the mountain was in two but the blast had caused the rocks to heat up charring the maize grains into colours of black, red, white and yellow.

So man had his maize grain with the help of the rain gods, but who were these rain gods? Most Mayan mythology comes to us from ancient codices written in the 11th Century which, although have a significant Spanish flavour from the conquests, provide us with an idea of Mayan cosmology. The Mayans had several deities covering all aspects of life and the most common factor among them was that each deity had four aspects to represent the four cardinal points. The rain gods were no exception to this.

The singular rain god was called Chac and was often described as having a reptilian face with a long downturned snout and two great fangs. He was great in stature and attended by small frogs whose croaking heralded his arrival. Following the Mayan principal of four aspects, Chac too had four: Chac Xib Chac (the red Chac of the East), Sac Xib Chac (The white Chac of the north), Ek Xib Chac (The black Chac of the west) and last, but not least, Kan Xib Chac (the yellow Chac of the south). The colours of the cardinal points were generally the same regardless of the deity but it's interesting to note that these colours are the same as the newly discovered charred maize grain.

The Chacs were believed to send rain by sprinkling water from calabashes, or gourds, that they carried. If the calabashes were all emptied at once the world would be flooded. The Chacs sent the rain but they also sent hail and long periods of damp that could ruin crops. The Chac therefore may be a beneficent deity or a death dealer. This is depicted nicely in one of the Mayan Codices which contains a picture of a Chac caring for a young tree, immediately behind is a death god who tears the tree in half.

Ritual formed a cornerstone of Mayan civilisation and honouring the Chacs was no exception. The Mayan calendar contained nineteen months, based on the aspects of the moon, and 3 of those months contained ceremonies dedicated to the Chacs.

In the months of Chen (the moon) and Yax (Venus) a great festival known as Ocna took place to honour the Chacs. Which month it was held would depend on the outcome of consulting the Bacabs gods – four gods closely associated with the Chacs. The Bacabs would determine the day of the ceremony. On the chosen day, the temple of the Chacs had a complete renovation, all the incense burners and idols were replaced and sometimes the temple was completely knocked down and rebuilt.

In the month of Mac (possibly meaning a young god) the ceremony of Tup'Kak took place to secure rain for the coming season and the maize. The month of Mac was roughly end March to early April just before the main rainy season. Before the ceremony a great hunt took place to capture live birds and animals. On the day a great fire was built and the creatures sacrificed and their hearts thrown into the fire. Four old men, representing each Chac, would then extinguish the fire and the rain gods were invoked with prayers and offerings. The offerings usually involved incense of which copal was highly favoured. Copal was harvested from trees as a resin and those trees which had been struck by lightning were considered especially sacred. The incense was often made into cakes and painted a turquoise blue, a colour considered sacred to the gods.

The concept of sacrifice was an important one in Mayan culture and human sacrifice to the rain gods also took place. If the rain gods were particularly angry then one way to pacify them was to throw people into a large cenote, a large deep water-filled sink hole where the roof has collapsed, where they would subsequently drown. These cenotes were considered to be entrances to the underworld where everyone's soul had to pass through before going to paradise. Deep caverns and caves were also considered to be entrances to the underworld but also the place where fertilising rains were created before being sent to the sky. Even today, modern Mayans perform ceremonies in caves just before the rainy season.

A ceremony to the Chacs is still held in the villages of the Yucatan today when rain is needed. Every man in the village attends. The first task is the collection of virgin water, from a cenote where women never go, for the food preparation. Once this has been done the men must not return home – if a man and women have intercourse the rains will not come. Therefore, the men depart the village and sleep in hammocks on the outskirts. After two days of preliminary ceremonies the shaman offers, at dawn on the third day, thirteen tall gourds and two shallow gourds of Balche, a mild intoxicating drink, to the Chacs. There is chanting and the Balche is distributed amongst those present who each take a little as it purifies one of evil. Four assistants to the Shaman then hold a bird by the wings and legs while the shaman pours Balche nine times down the bird's throats and dedicates them to the rain gods

– the birds are then sacrificed. Balche is then sprinkled thirteen times on the altar and each time it is offered to those present. By noon food is ready and the main ceremony can commence.

Four boys are then tied by their right leg to a post on the altar. The boys represent the small frogs who are the assistants and musicians of the rain gods. As the ceremony proceeds they croak like frogs heralding the approach of a storm. An older man, chosen to represent the elder rain god, is brought to the east of the altar. He is provided with a calabash and a wooden knife. The wooden knife represents the implement the rain gods use to create lightening. Every so often the older man makes a noise like thunder and brandishes the wooden knife. As an alternative the older man is replaced with four men each representing a Chac – each time the shaman offers prayers or Balche they dance around the altar.

The altar is piled with food and drink. Thirteen tall gourds, two shallow gourds, nine pails of broth from the sacrificed birds, nine piles of tortillas made of maize and squash seeds. All this food is offered to the rain gods and everyone departs so the Chacs can feast without interruption. After an appropriate time the shaman returns and anoints the Chac impersonators with more Balche. At which point the food is divided between those present (its spiritual essence removed by the gods) and the rain petition is concluded.

All the symbolism is an expression of magic – they are the expressions of the Mayan preoccupation with the living maize and the gods who nourish him and provide life-giving rain.

Bibliography

Sharer, Robert J. and Traxler, Loa P., *The Ancient Maya*. Stanford University Press, 2005.
Coe, Michael D., *The Maya (Ancient Peoples and Places)*. Thames and Hudson, 2005.
Thompson, J. Eric S., *The Rise and Fall of Maya Civilisation*. University of Oklahoma Press, 1985.

A Feast for Water

Baptism in the Thelemic Tradition

Rodney Orpheus & Cathryn Orchard

Water is one of the basic elements of life, and consequently also one of the most basic and widely-used elements in religious rites. Within the Thelemic tradition, Ecclesia Gnostica Catholica (the Gnostic Catholic Church) incorporates the element of water as a fundamental part of its ritual workings. A font of water is placed within the temple of the Gnostic Mass, the central rite of E.G.C., and the rite of baptism with water is celebrated. Most people in the Western world are familiar with baptism in the context of Christianity, but the practice is a great deal older.

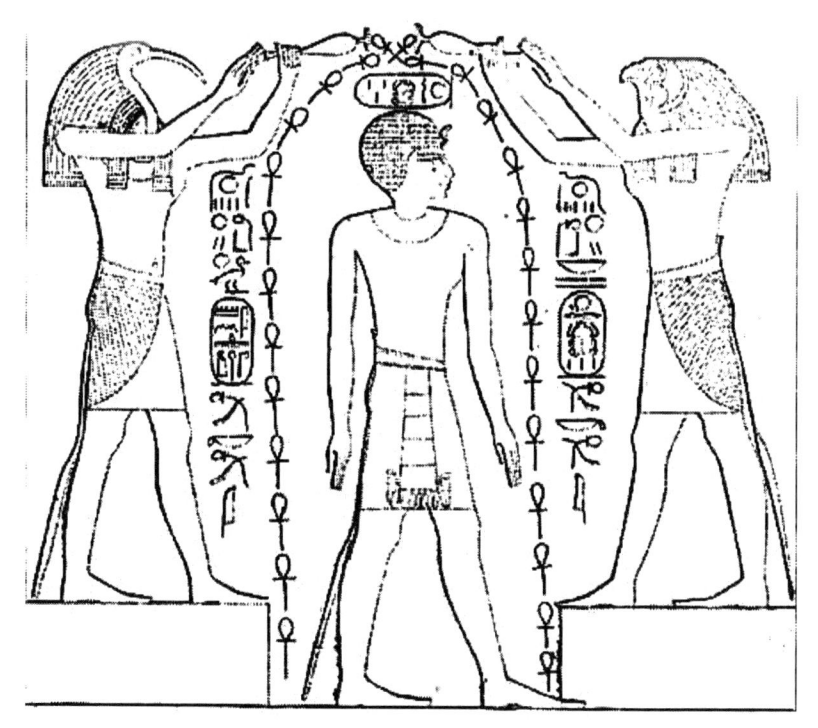

The baptism of Rameses II by Thoth and Horus

In Egypt, in ancient Heliopolis (the *'City of the Sun'*) the Pharaoh, who was the living manifestation of god on earth, would enter one of his private temples *'the House of the Morning'* at sunrise each day to be sprinkled with water. This act was a symbolic unification with the sun-god Ra, who was believed to be reborn at dawn via the waters after his journey through the night; just as human beings were reborn via the waters of the amniotic fluid. In a depiction at the temple complex in Karnak, the Pharaoh Rameses II is shown having water poured over him by the gods Thoth and Horus. As Professor Richard Gabriel notes in *Gods of our Fathers: the memory of Egypt in Judaism & Christianity* (2001):

> "...the water is depicted not with the hieroglyph for water, but with the ankh, the hieroglyph that is the symbol for life."

thus affirming that the essential notion is not simply of purification but also of rebirth. Gabriel further explains that:

> "Egyptian baptism was meant to prepare the recipient to enter into the presence of the god or ... to prepare the recipient to receive the god within him. Thus it was that through baptism one was "reborn" or made god-like or made worthy of union with the god."

Most Christians generally believe that baptism is necessary in order to purify the recipient from sin, but Jesus, who himself was supposedly without sin, insisted on visiting John the Baptist before he could begin his ministry. The *Gospel of Matthew 3:16* relates:

> "And Jesus, when he was baptised, went up straightway out of the water: and, lo, the heavens were opened unto him, and he saw the Spirit of God descending like a dove, and lighting upon him."

So again we see that baptism is used to prepare the candidate for the reception of divinity, and this story of Matthew's is quite possibly a reference to earlier Egyptian rites in order to show his contemporaries that Jesus was truly a manifestation of god, as were the Pharaohs. The early Christian writer Cyril of Jerusalem makes this concept of rebirth into godhood plain in his *Catechetical Lecture 20 (On the Mysteries Of Baptism)*:

> "After these things, you were led to the holy pool of Divine Baptism, as Christ was carried from the Cross to the Sepulchre which is before our eyes... And at the self-same moment you were both dying and being born; and that Water of salvation was at once your grave and your mother. [...] Let no one then suppose that Baptism is merely the grace of remission of sins ...we know full well, that as it purges our sins, and ministers to us the gift of the Holy Ghost, so also it is the counterpart of the sufferings of Christ."[87]

In other words, baptism in the Christian tradition is both a purification and a symbolic re-enactment of the mysteries of death & rebirth to allow the divine to enter into the candidate, just as it was to the Egyptians.

This rite of baptism was so important that early Christians would baptise new members in local springs and streams, frequently those which may have been previously considered sacred springs by pagan worshippers; but as churches became larger and more stable this custom was replaced by the construction of baptismal fonts - from the Latin word *fons* (*fontis*) meaning a *'fountain'*. It should thus be remembered that a font is symbolically a spring or fountain within the church, i.e. living flowing water, not static water - hence why is it normally a fixed pedestal, whence the sacred spring flows forth.

However tempting as it may be to see baptism as an original Egyptian rite transmitted to us via Christianity, it is important to note that baptism rituals were also practised by cultures with no discernible relationship to Egyptian or Judeo-Christian religious systems. Prescott (1843) describes a pre-Christian Mexican baptismal ritual that astounded the conquistadors with its similarity to those they knew; and 12th century Norse chronicler Snorri Sturluson describes baptism among pagan Scandinavians in his histories. So we can see the near-universal importance of baptism with water across all of humanity.

When Aleister Crowley was writing the Gnostic Mass circa 1913 (later used by Gerald Gardner as a foundation for his early witchcraft rituals in the 1950s) he included a font within the temple furnishings, acknowledging the importance of having the waters of a sacred spring within the rite. He also noted towards the end of the ritual:

---

[87] Catechetical Lecture 20. 4 & 6.

> "The PEOPLE communicate as did the PRIEST, uttering the same words in an attitude of Resurrection: "There is no part of me that is not of the Gods." The exceptions to this part of the ceremony are when it is of the nature of a celebration, in which case none but the PRIEST communicate; or ... part of the ceremony of baptism, when only the child baptised partakes..."

Thus clearly indicating that he felt that the newly-founded Gnostic Catholic Church should contain a ceremony of baptism, and that this ceremony should include the Gnostic Mass as a subsection.

Some years later, in 1921, Crowley made some diary notes toward how this baptism ritual should work:

Ideas about our baptismal ceremony
1. All born free -- quote Law.
2. [illegible]
3. CCXX about children.
4. Object of rite.
5. Address to mother, who abandons the Child & goes out.
6. Address to Godfathers and Godmothers, who swear to defend child's freedom and initiate it.
7. They swear this.
8. The Creed.
9. "I will" to this.
10. I will do my own will, etc.
11. Grant, etc.
12. Consecrates Water and wine.
13. Name child.
14. Baptize with Water.
15. Baptize with wine.
16. Reception
17. Pater Noster. / exhortation and applause.

We can see the conception of rebirth here once more, in that the Mother leaves the Child to the spiritual care of the Godparents, the Child is then named, baptised with water (and with wine, which is somewhat of an innovation) and received as a new member of the Church.

"*CCXX about children*" is a reference to verses spoken by the goddess Nuit in Crowley's Book of the Law:

> "*I 5. Help me, o warrior lord of Thebes, in my unveiling before the Children of men!*
>
> *I 12. Come forth, o children, under the stars, & take your fill of love!*
>
> *I 15. Now ye shall know that the chosen priest & apostle of infinite space is the prince-priest the Beast; and in his woman called the Scarlet Woman is all power given. They shall gather my children into their fold: they shall bring the glory of the stars into the hearts of men.*"

The word '*Children*' is here used in a very broad sense: Nuit refers to '*my children*', and we are all Children of the goddess - regardless of our physical age in this body.

Crowley commented on verse 12 that it was:

> "*The Key of the worship of Nu. The uniting of consciousness with infinite space by the exercise of love, pastoral or pagan love.*"

Just as the Pharaoh became divine by being united with our local star, the sun; and Jesus united with the Holy Spirit descending in the form of a dove; so does Thelemic baptism unite all of us Children of the New Aeon with the divine starry essence of the goddess of infinite space.

Bishops of E.G.C. Tau Helena & Tau Apiryon (2004) wrote:

> "*Thelema rejects the idea of original sin. So, for us, baptism represents a symbolic birth into the Thelemic community. The child heeds the call of Nuit, who declares, "Do what thou wilt shall be the whole of the Law." The child enters the portals of Her Church, where he or she is welcomed into the community of worshippers, leaving the profane world and its materialistic obsessions behind.*"

For Thelemites, baptism into E.G.C. is thus a rebirth into the Gnostic church, and, as Gabriel described in the Egyptian mysteries, a preparation to enter into the presence of the gods - in this case the godhood invoked within the Gnostic Mass.

Bibliography

Baring-Gould, S. *The Origin and Development of Religious Belief.* London: Rivingtons, 1869.

Crowley, Aleister. *The Old and New Commentaries to Liber AL.* http://www.hermetic.com/220/crowley-comments.html.

Gabriel, Richard A. *Gods of Our Fathers: The Memory of Egypt in Judaism and Christianity.* Greenwood Press, 2001.

Helena and Tau Apiryon. "The Invisible Basilica: Liber XV: The Gnostic Mass: Annotations and Commentary," July 10, 2004. http://www.hermetic.com/sabazius/gmnotes.htm#children.

Lewis, Abram. *Paganism Surviving in Christianity.* New York: G. P. Putnam's sons, 1892.

Peterson, John B. *Baptismal Font - Original Catholic Encyclopedia.* http://oce.catholic.com/index.php?title=Baptismal_Font.

Prescott, William. *History of the conquest of Mexico, with a preliminary view of the ancient Mexican civilization, and the life of the conqueror, Hernando Cortés.* New York: Harper, 1843.

Schaff, Philip, and Henry Wace, eds. *Nicene and Post-Nicene Fathers.* Vol. 7. 2. Buffalo, NY: Christian Literature Publishing Co., 1894. http://www.newadvent.org/fathers/310120.htm.

White, Jon Ewbank Manchip. *Everyday Life in Ancient Egypt.* Courier Dover Publications, 2002.

STRUNG LIKE PEARLS

DION FORTUNE'S SEA PRIESTESS AND ITS RELATIONSHIP TO THE ELEMENTAL CONTACTS OF WATER

BY DIANE M. CHAMPIGNY

Until my 26th year, I lived at the lip of an inlet on the Boston Harbor in Massachusetts. The energy of the sea was at my very doorstep. I felt the ebb and flow of her tides, was intoxicated by her unmistakable briny aroma, was in awe of her many moods and communed with her primordial intelligence. I was an only child and this mysterious elemental force with the grey-green mantle was my constant companion and guide. She proved to be an unceasing, infinite power overseeing creation and dwarfing all that is mortal. Healing, calming, nurturing, yet bitter, foreboding and cruel at the same time. I learned early on that the Great Mother has a dual nature that is neither positive nor negative, but is simply the fabric of creation. At the centre of creation is the unspoken promise that one wave will follow another in an endless cycle, and so it will always be. The ocean, the Great Mother, is that from which all life springs, and paradoxically is the tomb of all things. As it states in the Charge of the Goddess: *"From me all things proceed, and unto me all things must return."* Therein lies a profound mystery.

Water is symbolically associated with compassion, intuition, emotion, and the subconscious. As water is transformed when placed in a cup, water is formless and simultaneously forming. The seashore is a very liminal place and all liminal places are magickal. They act as doorways, portals and gates to other worlds. We can traverse the astral planes through them. Land, sea and sky meet here and it's just that type of atmosphere that is taken advantage of in *The Sea Priestess* by Dion Fortune.

The Sea Priestess was self-published by Dion Fortune in 1938. It is told in the first person from the diaries of Wilfred Maxwell, a London estate agent with dreams of escaping his humdrum existence. We are introduced to Dion Fortune's most beloved characters, Vivien Le Fay Morgan: Initiate of the Hermetic Path and Sea Priestess of Atlantis. She is in search of a location for her magickal experiments, and enlists Wilfred to find her the perfect location: an abandoned fort off a rocky headland. Wilfred also assists in the restoration and decoration of the property. There is tension in the air, as Wilfred inevitably starts to fall in love with Vivien, but the Sea Priestess keeps things on track by focusing on magickal goals. The Sea Priestess manipulates the relationship with Wilfred to produce magickal effects by sublimating or transforming the potential sexual energy to other channels. They work together as Priestess and Priest, scrying the *Fires of Azrael* and connecting with Vivien's inner contact, The Priest of the Moon. Certain obstacles in Wilfred's life are ultimately resolved; enabling him to enter into a satisfying relationship with Molly after the Sea Priestess takes her leave. Themes of ancient sea gods, sacrifice and synchronicity are explored. The significance of the ebbing and flowing of the magnetic tides of moon and sea are beautifully and evocatively illustrated. *The Sea Priestess* is a veritable treasure trove of metaphysical concepts and theory and a gold mine for ritual creation and construction.

The Goddess is symbolized by the elemental water triangle because water is a symbol of the sea, the primordial womb from which we all herald. She is of the seas and the starry heavens, which look like a celestial sea of amniotic fluid, whose veil is bespangled with stars.

The ocean is a sign of power and strength, dominating all other symbols of water due to its immensity. All life derived from this primordial soup, and life still exists in the ocean; therefore the ocean represents life.

The symbolism of water has a universal undertone of purity and fertility. Metaphorically, it is often viewed as the source of life itself as we see evidenced in countless creation myths in which life emerges from primordial waters. The wisdom of water is infinite, and you will find if you invest the time to contemplate its vastness you will be greatly rewarded.

Interestingly, we are all made of water, and so we can liken many of these myths and allegories to our own existence (the macrocosm mirroring the microcosm and vice versa.) Furthermore, we can incorporate the symbolism of circulation, life, cohesion and birth by associating the creative waters of the earth with the fluids found in our own body (i.e., blood.)

Dion Fortune states in the Inner Light Journal *"places tune mood, so it is well worth seeking the elemental contacts where they are present in their strength."* Locate an isolated shore and go there in the cooler months when few people are about. You can *'get there'* via the imagination just as well after initial contact is made and a sufficient rapport is built/established. Although a beginner needs all the help that physical conditions can provide, the experienced practitioner ought to be independent of them.

The true magickal direction of my life came about through my discovery of the writings of Violet Mary Firth, better known in occult circles as Dion Fortune. She was born on December 6, 1890 in Llandudno, North Wales. She derived her nom de plume from her family motto, which appeared on her family crest: *'Deo non Fortuna'* which is Latin for *'by God not fate.'* She subsequently shortened her new moniker to Dion Fortune.

She was an occultist, medium and author of the highest calibre. Her interest and involvement in psychoanalysis attracted her towards the occult by their perceptible overlap. She was brought up in a Christian Science household and was a member of the Theosophical Society and the Hermetic Order of the Golden Dawn before forming her own order, the Fraternity of the Inner Light, subsequently (and to this day) known as the Society of the Inner Light. The philosophical and practical line that Dion Fortune pursued throughout her life was a three-fold balance of those elements of the Western Esoteric Tradition that are sometimes called the Orange, Green and Purple Rays, in other words Hermetic Magick, Elemental and Nature Contacts, and Devotional Mysticism. She died of leukemia at the Middlesex Hospital, London on January 8th 1946, and is buried in Glastonbury – her beloved Avalon of the Heart.

I have a very personal relationship with Dion Fortune's work, which has played an important role in the cycles of my own development. Her work encourages personal revelation and the cultivation of the self; all-important milestones along the Path of Becoming. To think that she went out into the world on her own in the 1920's as a lone wolf and was able to forge the magickal legacy and current that she has is nothing short of amazing – a shining example of her intrinsic stick-to-itiveness, dogged perseverance and resolute tenacity. Occultists and pagans alike owe a great debt to her. I for one am honoured that I was brought to the Path through her work and esoteric knowledge.

Dion Fortune used the vehicle of the novel to present complex magickal and psychical theory. She was acutely aware of the spirit of place, which she often describes in great detail in her novels. *The Sea Priestess* features an outcrop of land that juts out into the Atlantic south of Bristol near Weston-Super-Mare. Dion Fortune herself described it as *'...shaped like a couchant lion with his tail into the sea.'* It is known as Brean Down (*'Bell Head'* in the novel.) Dion Fortune must have known Brean Down in the 1930s when the Victorian Fort had been converted into tearooms for wayfarers and tourists. The magickal drama in her novel is played out beyond the battlements at the very tip of the rocks. In a cave, its entrance appropriately facing West, is the secret dwelling of the Sea Priestess. It is in the context of this physical and legendary landscape that the Sea Priestess and her apprentice weave their mystic visions, which in turn form the channel/conduit for their magickal work.

> *"Dion Fortune saw Isis as the power that is veiled on Earth by the resplendent mantle of nature, but who can be visualized unveiled, in the starry heavens, in the radiance of the moon's reflected light. Thus does Vivien Le Fay Morgan appropriately evoke Isis at the time of the Full Moon."*[88]

There she raised her arms to the sky in the form of the horns of a crescent moon, to chant her evocation to Isis:

> *"O Isis, veiled on earth, but shining clear In the high heaven now the full moon draws near, Hear the invoking words, hear and appear Shaddai el Chai, and Ea, Binah, Ge."*

It is the people of Wales who gave Brean Down its name, for *Bryn* means 'hill' and it is there that Vivien Le Fay Morgan builds a temple dedicated to the powers of the sea and moon and enacts her Rite of Isis under the guidance of an inner plane contact known as the Priest of the Moon. Of this being Wilfred Maxwell states:

> *"The Priest of the Moon had personality in a very marked degree, and if he was a product of my subconscious, I am proud of it. There were times, not infrequent, when I used to wonder what*

---

[88] From The Occult Fiction of Dion Fortune by Gareth Knight, Thoth Publications, 2007

he was, and whether I was deluding myself, or whether I was loopy; but each time I met him afresh I knew what he was, beyond all doubting, and he left his mark on me."

The intention behind the magick of the Sea Priestess and her inner plane contact, the Priest of the Moon, was geared towards tapping the source of power connected to the inner tides of moon and sea. This is why they chose the deserted headland to establish a gateway between the planes. It is also not a twist of fate that the Sea Priestess chose the name Vivien Le Fay Morgan, with its mythical overtones connected to the Arthurian and Grail legends, which were very close to her heart. The work that they were performing in the novel is very much akin to the work that Dion Fortune and her small band of associates were embarking upon at the Chalice Well Club in Glastonbury. There, they made contact with their Inner Priesthood.

In real life Dion Fortune was a very powerful reality-based sorceress. Her books are designed as courses in genuine, true-to-life occultism that more than hint at occult motivation and experience. They describe the inner workings of an occult lodge from the inside. As she herself states, *"the Mystical Qabalah [her magnum opus] gives the theory, but the novels give the practice. Those who study the Mystical Qabalah with the help of the novels get the keys of the Temple put into their hands."*[89] Generous, sound advice if I ever heard it.

As Dion herself describes *The Sea Priestess*:

"It is a book with an undercurrent; upon the surface, a romance; underneath, a thesis on the theme: "All women are Isis, and Isis is all women," or in the language of modern psychology, the anima-animus principle."[90]

Vivien Le Fay Morgan is a Priestess of Isis in full incarnation, a worshipper of the sea and tides, the recognizer of the feminine principle in action on the earth. She is a Priestess of the cold sea cult of the primordial deeps. She taps into the deeper wisdom contacts where the earth and water meet; a liminal place indeed.

---

89 The Sea Priestess by Dion Fortune, Red Wheel Weiser, 2003 edition, page previous to Introduction
90 The Sea Priestess by Dion Fortune, Red Wheel Weiser, 2003 edition, from the Introduction.

The sea and its tides play a central role throughout the story, and are used to illuminate the tides, which surge within every human psyche. The ritual washing away of debris is seen as a spiritual crisis, which must be gone through before a pure result can emerge, saturated yet cleansed, on the other side. Much of the deep mystical meaning of this work is spelled out in no uncertain terms, the rest can be traced through meditation on the images and scenery drawn so well as the story unfolds. You would be spending your time wisely if you did so.

There is also the recurring theme of sacrifice running throughout the novel. Sacrifices of slaves bound alive to the rocks of the sea-cave, in honor of the Sea and the Great Goddess. The cult from which the Sea Priestess descended required living sacrifices. It is not lost on Wilfred that he has been chosen for this exact role. The *Fire of Azrael* was also considered an appeasement and tribute of earth to sea. Sacrifice/propitiation provide power, and you cannot get very far magickally without it. We gain magickal power to assist and support each other. It is a giving of the self as oppose to an actual ritual sacrifice. The *'idiot'* son of a worker who dies whilst building the structure for the Sea Priestess (known simply as the moon-calf) ultimately served as the sacrifice for the building of the sanctuary. The sea gods required a sacrifice in order to accept the fort as their Temple. Dion Fortune was committed to *'learning in order to serve'* and that is admirably illustrated in the novel's recurring theme of sacrifice. People genuinely involved in the Great Work view it as Service and Sacrifice and incorporate those principles into their daily lives. This lifts the burden for those who come after us and was of primary concern to Dion Fortune. She was doing the Work that she knew could never be finished in this lifetime, in the hopes that the next generation would pick up the baton and march forward with the Work.

The Moon and Sea simultaneously pull each other toward a balance achieved between periods of calm and storm. Holding opposite tensions produces creative acts: this book mirrors a High Priestess intending a spiritual psychodrama that creatively balances the masculine and feminine. In esoteric philosophy, the female is receptive/negative on the outer planes and active/positive on the inner planes, while the male is active/positive on the outer planes and receptive/negative on the inner planes. Each of us has both male and female elements within. It is interesting to note that the male and female roles change and interweave as you proceed from plane to plane, apparently to infinity. As far as Dion Fortune was concerned, the principle of polarity was one of the lost secrets of Western Occultism. Specifically, she selects a male to be the God to her Goddess as well as the time and place for the enfoldment. Both characters are willing participants, so the transformation is not an incident, but a process. *The Sea Priestess* places inner archetypal forces in the outer world. She created this book and others as practical applications of some of her metaphysical teachings. Everything in the book is like a dreamscape or active imagining filled with symbols and images we are able to incorporate into our own Workings.

A main point of the novel is the importance of creative imagination and the formation of an oscillatory circuit. Whether such visualization is objectively correct in lore or history is less important than the mutual intention of the pair of them to believe in it. As she states in the novel:

> "For me to make a magickal image by myself is auto-suggestion, and begins and ends subjectively. But when two or three of us get to work together, and you picture me as I picture myself, then things begin to happen. Your suggestion aids my auto-suggestion, and then it passes outside ourselves, and things begin to build up in the astral ethers, and they are the channel of forces."

What they were doing is creating astral forms to act as channels for spiritual/occult forces. This is the rationale behind the importance of the formation of a group mind in absolute rapport with itself. This type of work can be done within a small group of two or three people, or as a working partnership. This is the basis of magickal polarity work and has very little or nothing to do with physical sex, as is illustrated in the novel.

> "Isis Veiled is Our Lady of Nature. Isis Unveiled is the Heavenly Isis. Ea is the soul of space and parent of time. Ge, or Gaia, is the magnetic earth that forms an aura about the physical planet. Binah is the Great Sea of the Qabalah from whence all spiritual life arose, and beyond that the great Limitless Light of the Uncreate Realities from whence all creation springs."[91]

---

[91] The Occult Fiction of Dion Fortune by Gareth Knight, Thoth Publications, 2007.

I will close with one of the most evocative quotes from the book:

> "Behold we arise with the dawn of time from the grey and misty sea, and with the dusk we sink into the western ocean, and the lives of a man are strung like pearls on the thread of his spirit; and never in all his journey goes he alone, for that which is solitary is barren."

Bibliography

The Sea Priestess, Dion Fortune, Red Wheel/Weiser, 2003
The Occult Fiction of Dion Fortune, Gareth Knight, Thoth Publications, 2007
The Inner Light Journal (In house journal of the Society of the Inner Light)

Rituals of Water

By Magin

My background is in the Western Magickal Tradition and this essay reflects that; I ask those with a greater breadth of knowledge to make the necessary allowances. My intention is to consider some of the ways we use and experience water in a ritual context and what the reasons and interpretation of this might be. My definition of ritual is loose: broadly speaking I would define it as an action undertaken with meaningful intent – the ritual acts discussed in this article take place within a magickal or devotional context but that doesn't mean these are the exclusive context for *'ritual'* in our lives.

Like all the traditional elements water has both creative and destructive properties: the oceans take and give life; we need water to sustain us (and exist in it until birth), but we will drown if submerged for too long; water gives pleasure when we bathe and swim but its weight and power can crush almost anything in sufficient quantities; it fertilises the land but can also cause things to putrefy and stagnate. In all cultures we find tales about water: sea monsters threaten us, mermaids lure us, we are transformed within the cauldron, we drink to gain power and knowledge, we are sucked under and lost.

I will suggest that myth, legend, stories and histories about water serve to enrich and empower our use of it in a ritual context. Modern day notions of a tamed environment are therefore both impoverishing to our practice as well as being delusional. Water's mystery is that of surface and depth – it reflects back at us like a mirror but its surface is also the entrance to immense, mysterious depths. The treasures of both truth and the unknowable can therefore be sought through work with water. Our relationship with water is both one of potential pleasure and transformation and one of potential suffering and loss. When you turn on the tap to brush your teeth remember that the resulting water is the same water in which may be found mermaids, the Loch Ness monster, the kelpie, the kraken, the undine, the Nereide, the whale, the giant squid, the otter, the sardine, the anemone, the Titanic, the Viking funeral ship, and the lost city of Atlantis. In the words of the *National*

Geographic (1993) *"All the water that will ever be is, right now"*. It is the ultimate connector.

Water as Carrier

As you bathe before a ritual or sprinkle your working space with water to cleanse it, it is easy to feel familiar with water, to be comfortable with it. In my view water is often treated as a *'vehicle'* in ritual – it is instructed to cleanse, it washes away the bad, it brings in the good. In the womb water carries and protects us, in the ocean we ride upon it, on land we harness its might to grind corn and to generate power. In our modern lives we put chlorine, fluoride, mixers, bath oils, perfumes, teas and hundreds of other substances in water to make it more to our liking, to improve it as we see fit. In more religions, spiritual practices and magickal undertakings than can be listed here, water is used for personal purification prior to entry into sacred space or performance of a particular rite. In places of worship, ancient and modern, it is common to find a permanent supply of water available for worshippers to purify themselves with prior to entry, at designated times, or in preparation for a particular rite. Because of our knowledge of germs and the spread of disease it is easy to see these actions as being to ensure personal hygiene. Germs though were not the original target of pre-ritual purification which might be done to wash away physical impurity such as bodily fluids and food but might also purify the individual after certain activities including menstruation, sexual activity, contact with death and childbirth. Importantly, even if you have had a bath or shower you may still be required to perform your ablutions before ritual or prayer (signifying that the act of purification itself is important, not just how clean you are). For ritual purification holy water or water from a natural source is often prescribed or at least preferred, another indication that something else is going on in addition to the physical body being cleansed.

In Greek ritual the purified water (or lustral water) takes on the impurities of the space and is then placed outside of it.[92] Water might here be viewed as a scapegoat, carrying the impure and tainted away. On a larger scale we use water to do this for us every day when we flush out toilets and empty our baths. In traditions such as Wicca, which draw upon the *Key of Solomon,* water acts upon the astral realm,

---

92 Sophistes (2000)

cleansing and purifying that which is beyond the physical. Interestingly, it is necessary to exorcise the water itself first – meaning that the water is treated in a subtly different way to its earthy counterpart the salt, which is already considered pure. In the Christian tradition baptism is a single event where the soul is cleansed or exorcised and thus identified with Godhead (normally through the agency of the water itself though some creeds state that the actual immersion is merely a symbol of the repentance that has already occurred). In all of these cases water acts upon that which is beyond the physical; water, it seems can reach places other elements cannot.

Importantly, all of the ritual acts listed above either take place prior to or at the beginning of ritual, or serve to initiate/signify a new beginning. During ritual it is worthwhile noting when water is used and what its purpose is at that point in the proceedings. Water's presence as a purifier prior to or at the beginning of many ritual practices cannot be over-emphasised, as such, neither can its importance.

As a *'vehicle'* water is instructed and filled with intent that it then carries out either by purifying or taking on impurity. Although we associate purity with cleanliness and therefore health and wellbeing, it is important to remember that the act of purification sees water in its destructive aspect. Consider the story of Noah and his Ark.[93] In this story God causes water to purify the earth by means of the flood – the water destroys impurity. Noah has to make an Ark to save his family and the animals; it is God's will that they be saved but the water cannot be instructed to carefully skirt around the chosen few, that is not its nature. We often talk of *'unleashing the elements'* and it is as well to remember this when using them in ritual – a drop of water may seem harmless, but symbolically it may hold the full power and might of an ocean. It is also as well to remember that negative as well as positive energies may be carried by water (note that our water pipes and sewers are only beneficial to us if the water is flowing in the right direction). This may explain *The Key of Solomon*'s instruction to exorcise the water before using it – who knows where it has been and what it has done beforehand.

Before I finish the discussion of water as a *'carrier'* or *'vehicle'* I would like to mention the idea of the *'memory'* of water which was proposed by the immunologist Jacques Benveniste in 1988 (he wasn't

---

[93] Genesis 6-8, New King James Bible

responsible for the term itself). The notion of water carrying a memory of another substance it has previously mixed with builds on the idea of water as a vehicle – it will retain the nature of the substance it has encountered (whether positive or negative). We see this in the healing art of homeopathy and for all western medicine's protestations that this is nonsense, it cannot be denied that water has been used as a vehicle for *'concept'* (e.g. pure/impure) and faith healing techniques for age upon age. Water, it seems, has a special aptitude for taking on the energies and qualities it comes into contact with.

The Vessel that Overflows

The ability of water to carry our intentions to the astral and realms of the soul is also reflected in its counter-flow: the arts of psychism, dream work, mediumship and all forms of birthing where the new and unknown flow from us. Here we become the vessel that is filled and flowed through. Whereas when we purify water we seek to instruct it with our intent, here, we must learn to give up some of our control, to let the water take us where it will. These practices require one to open up, to step to one side, to allow the external and the subconscious to manifest. We might see this as the art of taking on the passive characteristics of water, but we might also see the nature of water itself becoming *'active'* and acting upon us. Wateriness and a ceding of control have both long-been associated with the feminine: a woman's body changes to some unseen rhythm (as do the tides), and during pregnancy she literally becomes a vehicle for new life (and a lot of water). Sexual energy is also connected with water, which is logical given the exchange of fluids that takes place. We might also note that when we feel intense grief or intense joy our bodies naturally produce water when we cry – we literally overflow with water as emotion wells up within us. While water is often considered to be a passive element, I do think it is important to consider and acknowledge its active qualities in our work. If we believe water to be a feminine element then it is not much of a leap to see why there are potential flaws in any characterisation that forces it into an exclusively passive role.

A practice that may initially seem to fit in more closely with that of water as *'vehicle'* is that of washing to renew virginity. In Greek myth both Hera and Aphrodite renew their virginity through bathing (Hera in a spring and Aphrodite in the sea). This event was often honoured through the washing of a statue of the goddess. Now, if we allow ourselves to be burdened by narratives where virginity is good and sex is bad, this might be seen as a *'purifying'* ritual, but there is no evidence that the Greeks saw it this way. Jane Ellen Harrison suggested that periodic renewal of virginity was simply seen as part of a cycle (note that Harrison also states that the virgin goddess Pallas Athene periodically renewed her virginity as a symbol of her continued maidenhood.)[94] For Hera and Zeus, this renewal allows them to encounter each other as if for their first time (and you can see why Aphrodite might have enjoyed this too). Zeus and Hera are then able re-initiate the *hieros gamos*, the sacred marriage that ensures the fertility of the earth. What we see here, therefore is not purification followed by contamination, but the fulfilment of a cycle that has water at its heart, both in the renewal of virginity and in the exchange of fluids that takes place at consummation – water literally creates, and flows through, the cycle of renewal and fulfilment.

In a dark twist on this Tacitus in his work *Germania* described how Nerthus, the Earth Mother, was annually bathed:

> *"Then the wagon and the hangings and, if you will, the goddess herself are washed clean in a hidden lake. Slaves perform this service, and the lake at once engulfs them: there is as a result a mysterious fear and a sacred ignorance about something seen only by those doomed to die."*[95]

Whether this was a statue or the goddess herself remains a mystery; we cannot know what the purpose of the bathing was, but if it did have similarities with the rites performed by the Greek goddesses, then death and sacrifice become woven into the pattern of life and renewal, and, once more, water is at the heart of the rite.

In Northern Europe *'receptive practices'* such as *seidr* magic were considered to be the precinct of women, as for a man to undertake them was to risk *'unmanning'*.[96] Water spirits are often depicted as female in Greek, Roman, Celtic and Anglo-Saxon myth and while some may heal such as Britain's Sulis and Coventina,[97] others bring danger such as the Greek Scylla and Charybdis,[98] and Grendel's mother in

---

[94] Harrison (1991) pp. 311
[95] Rives (trans), 1999, pp. 93
[96] Blain (2001)
[97] Green (1995)
[98] Graves (1992)

Beowulf.[99] We see the anxiety surrounding woman, water and the womb in nineteenth century concepts of hysteria and other predominantly female nervous disorders. As women moved into the sphere of learning, the professions and politics the resulting backlash was often couched in terms of what was *'natural'*, and how energy flowed – woman was literally believe to risk her womb withering as energy was diverted to her less well-developed brain.[100] Although not couched in mythic terms, woman takes on monstrous qualities – particularly when she attempts to move beyond her 'natural' watery realm. The stereotypes of the angel in the house and mad woman in the attic were the nineteenth century equivalent of the chaste, watery nymph and the insatiable she-monster of the sea.

A vast body of work exists concerning the *'othering'* of woman and her associations with danger, madness, the illogical and inexplicable during the nineteenth century and it is too large a topic to cover here.[101] It seems to me, however, that the facets of human existence that we associate with water – emotion, dream, the subconscious, the collective unconscious - have a way of resurfacing, no matter how much we attempt to suppress them. For all its passivity, water is immensely powerful and will not be suppressed. We cannot quash it (hence the marvels of hydraulics) and, if we attempt to, it will undoubtedly burst out in destructive ways – clearing away (purifying) that which seeks to suppress it.

We often look to the distant classical and pre-classical past as a way to weave meaning into our practice, as if the modern world is sterile of the riches the past has to offer us. I would suggest western society tends to compartmentalise, to differentiate fact and fiction, science and religion, truth and personal truth, thus making it difficult for us to interpret and manipulate the stories of our own lives – we break down experience so as to understand it and so reduce our ability to *'meaning make'* in a creative way. The mysteries of water teach us to make connections, to allow flow from one thing to another, to abandon our rigid ways. Perhaps we find it is easier for us to weave meaning from material drawn from the past as we don't feel the same compulsion to establish its factual accuracy before using it. Note how

---

99 Heaney (1999)
100 Drew (2002)
101 See Showalter (1987) and Gilbert and Gubar (2000) for a helpful introduction to this topic.

our main concern with the Loch Ness monster is not its nature but whether it is actually there or not, similarly, the scientific community continues to bang its head against any notion that homeopathy works because it is not currently possible to prove why it might work.

Yet the films we watch become more and more fantastical and horrifying, as if our lack of the mythic in our lives demands to be compensated through even more dramatic fantasy. If the Lady of the Lake were to rise up and throw Excalibur at a passing stranger next week you can be sure that the inquiry would focus its attention on dragging the lake, not on considering why she chose this point in time to do it; moreover, the unfortunate object of her projectile would probably be sectioned and the general population would subject him to ridicule (and yet still watch a film on the same subject with utter enjoyment and no sense of irony). I believe it is a mistake to neglect the present and its potential for meaning-making as to do so is to reinforce the divide between *'fact'* and *'fantasy'* which goes against the flowing, connective nature of water.

In the more recent past our literature teems with beautiful stories that can enrich and deepen our understanding of water. Shakespeare's *Ophelia*, Anderson's *Little Mermaid*, Tennyson's *Lady of Shallot* all have lessons about the nature of love, suffering and their relationship with water. These figures are as familiar to the modern reader as Poseidon or Aphrodite. The Romantic poets were well known for endowing nature with human characteristics and many of their poems feature water – the element being particularly suited to this form because of its ability to *'mirror'* us and so help our inner growth and transformation.

In the twentieth century we see the development of the *'stream of consciousness'* literary style (the term being coined by William James in 1892). Writers attempted to depict the 'stream' of an individual's mind within their writing, producing a fascinating art form which sought to be ultra-real (by presenting what is happening in the mind) but often ended up being quite surreal as *'meaning'* can often be lost in the stream of words and thoughts that are presented without interpretation or structure (the final chapter of Joyce's *Ulysses* being a fine example).

Robert Drewe uses the term *'hydrous psyches'* to describe writers who not only wrote about the sea but seemed to have a deep personal relationship with it.[102] He includes the Romantics poets and Virginia

---

102 Drewe (2009)

Woolf, amongst others, in this group, and you can feel the pull of water and the fascination it had for these literary giants[103] – there is certainly no lack of available material to help us plumb the depths of meaning that water may hold. The importance of these works for ritual practice lies in a nurturing of our own ability to become receptive; to be open and able to express the wisdom we receive through creative process. The technological advances of our society and championing of scientific inquiry can work to deepen the rift between fact and fiction, actuality and fantasy, making it harder for us to view *'story'* as anything other than entertainment. Yet it is through story that we build meaning, not through fact, and without meaning our ritual has no power.

The Healing Waters

Water can be heated or cooled to suit our pleasure and whim. Relatively speaking, it is not long since the family bath was a ritual in itself with a hierarchy of who went first with the last person probably not emerging much cleaner then they started. Communal sanitation has long been a civic concern with bathing houses, viaducts and arrangements for sewage being at the heart of our ability to build bigger and bigger cities without the population dying off. It is easy to forget that automatically heated water is still the luxury of richer populations. That isn't to say that enjoying hot water should be a guilty pleasure, just that the sanitation and comfort it provides should not be taken for granted. At the other end of the spectrum, cooled water and ice were even more difficult to find than hot water in days gone past - unless Mother Nature provided them. Ice and snow feature heavily in myth originating in Northern Europe and the experience of jumping from a sauna out into the snow or plunging into ice water is lauded by many. Taking pleasure in water as it features in our every day rituals is one of the ways we can empower our use of it in magickal ritual. As mentioned above, some of the greatest literary works about water were produced by *'hydrous psyches'*. Even better than reading a lyric poem about water produced by someone else, is building a personal relationship with water yourself, creating your own *'hydrous psyche'* (though

---

[103] See for example Woolf's The Waves and To the Lighthouse, Samuel Coleridge's The Rime of the Ancient Mariner, Henry Vaughan's The Water-fall, Algernon Charles Swinburne's A Channel Crossing and The Swimmer's Dream, John Keats Bright star, would I were Steadfast as Thou and Walt Whitman's On the Beach at Night Alone and "Out of the rolling ocean the crowd"

perhaps without quite as much melodrama or tragedy). In this way you establish your own unique connection with the element.

Healing by water may mean different things depending on whether we see water as a vehicle (carrying the latent memory of another substance that might harm us if physically present), or as having healing properties itself. The two are not mutually exclusive and healing work may benefit from both; but it is worthwhile remembering that one treats water as a beneficial *'delivery mechanism'* that we control (albeit that this is a unique property in itself), while the other sees water acting upon the sufferer in its own right.

The flow of water from one place to another holds great power and potential for transformation, but only if we reflect water's qualities within ourselves. The scientist who pours water from one beaker to another seeks to be objective, to keep the self separate from the experiment. The scientist will say, rightly, that a space sprinkled with water does not become cleaner, that a dream has no bearing upon the external world, that a bath only relaxes the muscles and allows the mind time to think. The person who is separate from the actions of water does not flow with it, does not allow the self to be the vehicle and is therefore not part of the experiment; therefore no transformation of self or surroundings will occur – there is no ritual without a practitioner. The mysteries of water are to do with the unseen, the hidden depth, that which is beneath the surface; they require a leap of faith, a trust in intuition and imagination. Perhaps our very ability to control water without having to think about it dulls our senses and means that we have to look for meaning in far away myth and complex symbol rather than in the recent past and our own direct experience. To experience the wonder and majesty of water we visit Niagara Falls, go scuba diving, take a cruise or perhaps swim with dolphins – we create a sense of occasion, a meaningful event. Perhaps we are trying to recapture a sense of wonder which we have lost due to water's instant accessibility in our everyday lives?

If wonder is only accessible to you when you access it in a non-ordinary way, then it is going to be very difficult for you to access that feeling of wonder when you perform ritual (inhibiting your ability to empower your rite). I have suggested that we need to allow water to act upon us, but if a ritual act is one performed with meaningful intent, then we must be able to reverse that flow, to gather the force and power of our experience with water and hone it at the point where we discharge our intent. In the same way that the scientist who acts upon water while remaining separate from the experiment will experience no effect on the self; so a powerful experience of water where we are only passive spectator may not be a transformative or meaningful experience to us.

Anodea Judith connects the Svadhistana chakra (in the abdomen, associated with the element of water) to the physical memory of the body.[104] It is through this watery chakra that powerful physical memories may be awakened and re-experienced. I can attest to the literal truth of this statement in that I tested the theory by taking a bath (without having a book to hand as I would normally do), and allowed myself to fully feel whatever memories and associated emotions washed to the surface. The power of my experience was intense and surprising. Obviously this is a deeply personal thing but that is what makes it so precious and I can only recommend that you try it for yourself; you may have more success in the rain, the sea or a natural pool – whatever works for you. What the experience taught me was an appreciation of the power of water itself, no associations, no weaving of story and narrative around it was necessary. Following on from the experience I have felt that my relationship with and use of water in ritual practice is more focused, more empowered and more connected to the actual presence of the water rather than what I think it should be doing.

The experience of water can be a healing one for all people, after all we all started out in water. Standing in the rain or in running water can be deeply cathartic, as we allow the water to wash away our cares and our troubles (bringing us back to the idea of water as a purifier); immersing ourselves in warm water is both physically soothing and can bring deep healing and inner transformation, while ice water is invigorating, renewing, not to mention brilliant to drink on a hot summer's day.

Many people will make special trips to particular water sources in order to find healing and these same sources may be used to collect water for the purification of sacred spaces or for consumption (where it is safe to do so). These pilgrimages assume that the water carries something particularly special, hearkening back to the idea of water as a vehicle for other things. In healing rituals, therefore, water may be used to achieve different ends depending on individual need.

The Gift

I want to conclude with the gifts we exchange with water. Consider the concept of the wishing well – we make an offering and ask that our wish be granted. Because of its physical properties, water is especially suited to gift giving. The gift is not immediately destroyed as it might be with fire, and (unless the water is shallow), we cannot get it back as we would be able to do if we bury it – the gift sinks down into the depths and is lost to us. If the water is clear then we can watch our gift slip away from us and once it has disappeared we can only guess at where it might end up. Pools sacred to a particular spirit or deity may be filled with hundreds and thousands of votive offerings as well as wishes (or often curses) which the giver hopes will come to be. Once again, water is being asked to carry out our intention, but in this instance we make an offering or sacrifice to it in exchange for our wish.

In our environmentally conscious age it can seem wrong to throw things into water, and I certainly wouldn't recommend chucking great armfuls of gifts into the depths. I would also question the intention behind (and the likelihood of your desire being fulfilled by), throwing synthetic or harmful material into water. In general an offering such as food, drink or a biodegradable material is good for marking occasions and generally paying your respects. For a more solemn occasion the power of offering something precious to you cannot be denied and the link between yourself and the water source will feel particularly powerful in future as the water retains your offering. Remember when you next do the washing up, soak your feet after a long day and step forward to be purified with water, that that same water that touches you now may have touched your offering, wherever it may be.

Bibliography

Blain, Jenny, *Nine Worlds of Seid-Magic.* Routledge, 2001.
Drew, Robert, *The Penguin Book of the Beach*, Penguin, 2002.
Gilbert, Sandra M. and Gubar, Susan. *The Mad Woman in the Attic*, Yale Nota Bene, 2000.
Graves, Robert. *The Greek Myths*, Penguin, 1992.
Green, Miranda. *Celtic Goddesses*, British Museum Press, 1995
Harrison, Jane Ellen. *Prolegomena to the study of Greek Religion.* Princeton University Press, 1991
Heaney, Seamus. *Beowulf*, Faber and Faber, 1999
Joyce, James, *Ulysses*, Picador 1997.
Judith, Anodea, *Eastern Body, Western Mind.* California: Celestial Arts, 2004
Larson, Jennifer, *Greek Nymphs.* Oxford University Press, 2001.

---

104 Judith (2004) pp. 103-163

Moore, Thomas, *Care of the Soul*. Piatkus Books, 2008.
Rankine, Davie and d'Este, Sorita, *Wicca Magickal Beginnings*. Avalonia, 2008.
Rives, J.B. (translator), Tacitus, *Germania*, Oxford University Press, 1999.
Showalter, Elaine *The Female Malady*, Virago, 1987
Sophistes, Apollonius, *Hellenic Magic Ritual*, 2000
http://www.cs.utk.edu/~mclennan/OM/BA/HMT/
National Geographic, October 1993
New King James Bible
The Poetry Foundation www.poetryfoundation.org

WATER: A KEY TO HEALING

BY HARRY BARRON

The Moon is a wondrous object that is a both a source of illumination and a body of fascination that is suspended in the heavens above us. When it is at its fullest, we are compelled to stop and gaze up at its beauty in awe and marvel. And we attempt to ritually attune ourselves to its tides and seasons, a feat that magickally inclined people do routinely, as they proceed on their numinous quests and pursuits of the mysteries of the invisible world. The Moon has a subtle effect on the landscape, bathing it in a dim, yet gothic, fey and ephemeral radiance. And its effects on living and breathing creatures, both animal and plant, are almost supernatural. We are told that the insane respond aggressively to the baneful glare of the Moon and the police often report an increase in violent crime during the reign of that Silvery Disk. Just look at all the superstitions and folklore that have arisen around the Full Moon: vampires, werewolves, witches' sabbats and so forth. But we have to ask ourselves whether it is the Moon itself that causes these mental disturbances, or whether it is another substance that is being influenced that causes them. Impressive as the Moon's appearance is in the starry-lit sky is, it seems that Water is the main factor that we need to consider.

Water is an important part not just of our planet, as the greater part of our world is covered by Water, but it is also a major part of our physical constitution. It is said that from the Depths we have come and indeed, Water constitutes between 65% and 90% of cells in the human body. Consequently, astrologers, mystics and physicists deem that the Moon has a measurable effect on the Water in the body, as indeed it does on the tides of the seas and oceans. The Moon affects the Water within our bodies and the chemicals that flow within the waterways that are our cardiovascular and lymphatic systems. But it is not really the Moon I wish to discuss here, although I am always in awe of its majesty whenever I see it in the dark sky, but Water, that liquid element, vessel of mystery and grail of emotion. And Water holds one of the keys to healing us of our ailments and ills.

I remember that when I first became interested in holistic healing over 20 years ago, I started attending weekend seminars in World's End, Chelsea, London, where we learned how to harness the electrical power of the body for health and healing. One of the exercises we were given in order to promote our own healing was to charge a glass of water with our own auric energy and then drink it. Many were understandably sceptic, so we were encouraged to perform an experiment: two glasses were filled with water from the same source, but one glass was placed to the forehead and we were taught to consciously will the water to be full of healing energy. Then two tomatoes we placed into the glasses, preferably from the same vine, one into each glass; one going into the charged water and the other going into the uncharged water. And then you left them on a windowsill for a week or two...

At the next meeting, people came in eager and excited to share the news of how their experiments had gone and how their tomatoes were. Most of the people conducting the experiment had found that the tomatoes in the charged water remained in a good and healthy state and had not spoiled; whereas the tomatoes placed into the uncharged water, withered and rotted, as you might expect under normal circumstances. People were astounded. If this is the effect that charged water has on a tomato, imagine what effect the charged water would have on the body!

In more recent times, a Japanese scientist, Dr Masaru Emoto (*Messages from Water: 1999*) and a Persian physician, Dr Fereydoon Batmanghelidj (*Your Body's Many Cries for Water: 1992*) have carried out notable research on the properties of water. Dr Fereydoon Batmanghelidj had been imprisoned at the start of the Iranian Islamic revolution at the end of the 1970's and had been sentenced for execution. However, that sentence was never carried out, as Dr Batmanghelidj was placed in charge of caring for the prison's sick inmates and it was during this time that he discovered the healing properties of water. When there was no medicine available, he made his patients sip water as a form of medication and was astonished to watch their recovery. He was eventually released from prison and carried out more research and published books and articles about his findings. Although his discoveries have not been adopted by the general medical establishment, this does not mean to say that what he has been teaching is invalid, seeing how much the body is made up of water.

Dr Masaru, on the other hand, investigated the effects of thoughts and emotions on water. He charged the water by writing either positive words such as *'love'* or by negative words, such as *'hate'* on the container that held the water, or by influencing the water with similar positive or negative thoughts. He then froze the water and photographed the resulting crystals with a powerful electron microscope. The water charged with positive words and emotions showed beautifully formed patterns of harmonized crystals, whereas the water charged with negative emotions showed frightening, chaotic and ugly shaped patterns in the crystalline structure. Of course there was always a control: water from the same source that had not been charged with any emotion and the crystals always remained unformed.

Scientists are now saying that water holds memory, so the findings of Dr Masaru are unsurprising, but it does make you wonder about how we take water for granted. And if water does indeed hold such properties, then imagine the effect our emotions have on our own physical beings. If we are full of self-loathing and discontent with our lives, then that emotion will be held in our body. Many healers like to use the word *'dis-ease'* instead of *'disease'*, meaning that disease is caused by disharmony, not dissimilar to the philosophy of Traditional Chinese Medicine, which describes the process of illness as imbalances between Yin and Yang and which seeks to correct these imbalances to promote harmony within the organism. With the body being targeted by disharmonious emotions, it is almost inevitable that *'dis-ease'* will appear. If we change our emotions to positive ones, then surely those vibrations will change the state of harmony to dispel the *'dis-ease'* and bring about balance.

Another popular teaching that has been circulating recently is that of the *'Law of Attraction'*. If indeed there is such a Law, then our negatively charged bodies would act as a magnet to attract negative events and circumstances. By charging the water in our bodies with positive emotions, then surely that would change the polarity of what we are attracting into our lives and would bring us a more fulfilled existence by attracting only good and harmonious circumstances. As a by-product, this would bring about healing of any *'dis-ease'* or at least start the process of healing.

In many esoteric traditions, Water is seen as the mother of life. There are numerous sea Goddesses that are venerated throughout the world, Yemanyá being a well-known one from the Latin countries. We talk of being immersed in waters for cleansing rituals and healing: sacred wells such as St Winifreds in Holywell, North Wales, and Lourdes in France being two of many sacred water places, and there are many springs and holy wells around the world that have been recorded as having healing properties. This is often due to the mineral contents of the water but sometimes the healing seems to be a bit more esoteric, and indeed we cannot ignore the deep spiritual connection to water and health, especially at these shrines.

It is not possible to discount religious and spiritual rites performed in water, and while they may not strictly be for healing purposes, they do promote a sense of spirituality and that cleansing process can lead to rebalance in lives and as a consequence start the healing process. In Christianity, we find baptism, where the waters wash away the sins of the new believer. In Orthodox Judaism, there is the Mikva, the ritual bath usually in the depths of the synagogue, in which women wash away their impurities after menstruation and childbirth and into which new converts are immersed, symbolically entering a new life. In Islam the symbolic washing of the hands and feet before prayer and in Hinduism, the sacred rites performed in the sacred waters of the Ganges. In Wicca and other Mystery School rites water is mixed with salt, reforming the connection to the oceans, and is used to cleanse and consecrate a circle. Water is part of our spiritual heritage and its qualities and properties seem to be hidden deep within our conscious and subconscious beings.

Water is everywhere, it is part of us, and we are part of it, and with it, we can bring about change and healing.

THE MOON

THE DOOR OF DREAMS, AND THE TIDES WITHIN

BY MELISSA HARRINGTON

> "Our Lady is also the Moon, called of some Selene, of others, Luna, but by the wise Levanah, for therein is contained the number of her name. She is the ruler of the tides of flux and reflux. The waters of the Great Sea answer unto her, likewise the tides of all earthly seas, and she ruleth the nature of woman. But there is likewise in the souls of men a flowing and an ebbing of the tides of life, which no one knoweth save the wise; and over these tides the Great Goddess presides in her aspect of the Moon. She comes from the sea as the evening star, and the magnetic waters of the earth rise in flood. She sinks as Persephone in the western ocean and the waters flow back into the inner earth and become still in the great lakes of darkness wherein are the moon and stars reflected. Whoso is still as the dark underworld lake of Persephone sees the tides of the Unseen moving therein, and knoweth all things"
>
> (Fortune 1989: 203-204).

The passage quoted above is taken from *The Sea Priestess*, by Dion Fortune. The story is of a man called Wilfred, who finds his magic and manhood awakened by a powerful female magician, Morgan le Fay. Morgan is engaged in magical workings for the greater good of mankind, and recruits Wilfred as her Priest. The magical journey on which she takes him is one of discovery, in which Dion/Morgan reveals her cosmic doctrine about the tides of human consciousness, of life, of magic, and of the universe. This is evocatively imparted in prose, poetry and ritual, and is one of the best loved novels in the occult genre.

Fortune's literary work frequently stresses the mystery of the ebbing and flowing of the tides of the cosmos, and their import to humanity. In common with many of her contemporary ceremonial magicians, theosophists and pioneers of the new age, she believed in new frontiers of human consciousness, and the place of magic in bringing that to birth. She was versed in the teachings of the Golden Dawn, and founded the Society of Inner Light, as well as writing many popular books on esoteric philosophy.

Fortune's stressing of *'the tides'* is not unusual amongst teachers of magic, whether that refers to the greater tides or the lesser tides of cosmic lore. On a basic level these are ruled by the movement of the sun, moon and stars, and it is not for nothing that the traditional image of the wizard is of an old man with a gown covered in stars and moons, or that the magi at the heart of the Christian myth travelled by the light of a great star.

Once such teachings were prized secrets, but today, thanks to the birth of the printing press, of modern technology, and now the internet, most of the information needed to work with the tides of the cosmos is but a click away. However it is still rare to find many modern magicians who work according to the strict tables of angelic hours, or draws up astrological charts to obtain optimal success in their workings. Many contemporary Pagan workings are done in a rather ad hoc fashion according to the basic interaction of the solar cycle of the eight Sabbats, and the ebbing and flowing of the lunar cycle. This is probably sufficient for most work, and with the ever growing ethical dimensions of magic today it is unlikely that the plethora of healing rites that get performed, alongside basic creative visualization, can lead the practitioner to much harm, or to bitter results.

Thus in these modern times the moon has perhaps even more significance than she used to in magical workings. For many of us, just as for the fictional Wilfred, the Moon and her magnetic pull holds the keys to our entry to the world of magic, and its own ancient science. The moon is very much the *'door of dreams'* by which we enter the worlds of the subconscious, of the collective unconscious, the mystical etheric realms in which the physical world fades away from our attention, and other worlds and ways of being come to light.

Magicians have long used the Kabbalah as a map of the universe, and a system with which to understand esoteric philosophy. In esoteric Kabbalah Yesod is the sphere (*sephirah*) associated with moon, and sited above Malkuth, the earthly sphere. Yesod is known as the ninth path, and is also known as the foundation, as well as the vision of the machinery of the universe, and the treasure house of images. Yesod is the receptacle of the emanations of the higher *sephiroth*, gently shedding its light on the earthly sphere below, acting as the first doorway for the magician to *'rise on the planes'*.

Kabbalistically Yesod may be associated with the moon, but the waters of life, and of death, are in Binah, the bitter sea we must all traverse one day. This *sephira* links, via the path of Daleth, *'the door'*, to Chokmah, the preceding, and complementary, *'male' sephira*. Daleth is a path portrayed in popular Tarot as the Empress, painted in the ubiquitous Rider-Waite pack as the fecund, star-crowned corn Goddess. Each *sephira* is receptive to the one preceding it. As the bright fertile mother Aima, the great mother Goddess conceives us with the explosive potential generated by Chokmah; as the dark mother Ama she imprisons us in flesh, and brings us, via birth, to mortality. As Dion Fortune points out, the gates of life are the gates of death, for they bring force into form, and the gates of death are the gates of life for they bring form into force once more.

Vivianne Crowley's *A Woman's Kabbalah* contains some lovely poetry and excellent exercises for teaching/learning western esoteric Kabbalah, and includes this poem in its chapter on Binah (Crowley 2000:57):

> *"Blessed Be the Great Mother,*
> *Without beginning and without ending.*
> *Blessed Be her temple of pure black marble,*
> *Blessed Be the stillness of her holy place.*
> *Blessed Be the wave that caresses the shore for her,*
> *Blessed Be the sand that succumbs to its embrace,*
> *Blessed Be the shell that is cast up from her,*
> *Blessed Be She the Mother of Pearl,*
> *Blessed Be She*
> *Blessed Be."*

The moon and the ocean are potent forces on which to meditate. As Binah can be glimpsed in the vast darkness of the ocean at night, so Yesod can be seen in white portal of the moon, one of the most easily understood symbols of a doorway into the great celestial spaces. Whilst our own earth planet is spinning round the sun we do not consciously see or feel it move, but the moon is ever present and ever changing. Within a short month we can all see the bright moon wax to full, then wane. We can note the darkness in which the moon is reborn, then enjoy the bright crescent of hope that is the first sight of the next moon cycle to come.

In most cultures it has not gone unnoticed that woman's approximate 28-day menstrual cycle mirrors the moon cycle, which is why menstruation is called just that, linked by etymology to the moon and the month. Thence some contemporary Pagan paths have embraced the image of a threefold Goddess whose faces reflect the ages of women and the phases of the moon, and incorporated her into our rites. Pagans are keen to facilitate empowering rites for girls who are coming in to the blessing of fertility, codifying the onset of menstruation as a celebratory rite of passage, rather than the unspoken curse of womankind. We also have croning/crowning rites for women to celebrate the end of menstruation and fertility, celebrating keeping the *'wise blood'* within them, and acknowledging their status as elders in the community. We aim to mark these tides in our lives alongside the more usual rites of passage.

Mankind has always marked the seasons and used the movement of the celestial bodies as a guide for navigation, planting, and agricultural affairs. Bioorganic farmers today recommend planting by solar and lunar cycles, and not just in trendy suburban allotments concerned with eco saintliness. The paragraph below regarding lunar planting rhythms is from a website for biodynamic farmers in India:

"Perhaps the most familiar is the rhythmic movement from New Moon to Full Moon that we witness each month. This is only 1 of numerous lunar or moon rhythms that astronomy scientists have mapped and can accurately calculate. The biodynamic farmer works primarily with 6 different moon rhythms that recur every 27-29 days. The Planting Calendar indicates the important days for farming activities during these 6 different rhythmic cycles each month.

The 6 Moon Rhythms are:
Full-New Moon   29.5 days
Moon opposite Saturn   27.3 days
Ascending-Descending Moon 27.3 days
Moon Nodes   27.2 days
Perigee-Apogee   27.5 days
Moon in Zodiac Constellations 27.3 days"
(http://www.biodynamics.in/Rhythms.htm)

The effect of the magnetic pull between the earth and the moon is most obvious in the ocean tides. The vast expanses of the seas that cover so much of our planet respond to the forces exerted by the rotation of the earth-moon system, in conjunction with gravity. Their movement offers us clear sight of the rhythms of our planet, and its orbit in the greater solar system. Thus it is not surprising that there are cross cultural myths about the effect of the moon on human beings, from the werewolf's howl to the lunatic's madness; nor that some urban folklore of this legendary effect attributes it to our watery nature.

We are born of water. Conceived in a cosmic burst of light we mirror the birth of our planet as we gestate in the womb. We are without form and yet from the void cells replicate and a foetus emerges from its own genetic primordial soup, to incarnate with unique fingerprints, unique mind and unique contribution to the human race. Our first sustenance is liquid, drawn from our mother's blood, and after birth, milk from her breast. Without food, or with very limited food, we can survive for relatively a long period of time, but without water we die quickly.

The human being is more than 60 % water. Bones hold approx 22%, brain and organs 75% and blood is 92% water. Water is necessary for all functions, transmuted from $H2O$ to synovial fluid, blood, plasma and lymph to transport oxygen and nutrients, and to urine, perspiration and even the moisture of our breath to transport waste products from our bodies. Babies have more water than adults and in old age we wither and dry, our life wizening from bouncing baby to wrinkled senior citizen. Thus beauty is related directly to how much water we have in our bodies, how our hair is luscious, our skin dewy, our eyes sparkling, with women throughout the planet trying to stave off the inevitable via creams and potions to rehydrate skin and hair.

Klauss Peter Endrees, and Wolfgang Schad wrote the book *Moon Rhythms in Nature: how lunar cycles affect living organisms*. Much of the book looks at worms and small creatures, and shows small but consistent lunar effects. However, these lecturers in evolutionary biology also looked at lunar effects on humans and found amongst other things, that pneumonia and eclampsia increased with a waxing moon. They examined the hypothesis that the full moon heralds the 'lunatics' in the asylum getting restless, and increased cases suicides and murder. The few scientific studies and correlations available proved that this is a much more complex area than had been previously realised, no one strong general effect was found, and confounding effects were noted at other moon phases, indicating that much more work could be done on this fascinating area of research.

The work of such scientists as Endrees and Schad is vital to our understanding of our planet and all its denizens. But it is probably in the discipline of psychology that most ground can be gained looking at the lunar and watery aspects of *homo sapiens*. The ancient Greek models of the four humours of mankind fit neatly into Jungian and transpersonal models of consciousness. Images of water often emerge in dreams and meditations as a representation of the unconscious, with forgotten or repressed 'things' lurking in its dark uncharted depths.

The liminal realms of our conscious can also correlate to the liminality of watery realms such as estuaries and tidal areas. We leave pits of mental quick-sand in places we least expect, where past traumas have not been processed, or where unresolved issues may suck us down into rumination and unspoken reproach. We experience rushes of anger, or love that may be beyond our own control, and we feel tides in our emotions. We can drown in our own thoughts, and be overtaken by our own emotional tidal waves that we can never out-run.

Myth is rich in imagery about gaining that holy grail, that fountain of eternal life, or that elixir of everlasting youth. It is not without good reason that the grail quest has such a place in mythic folklore, or that in the Arthurian myth cycle the Lady of Lake has such an important place, and that Excalibur is returned to her lake. It is no coincidence that Gabriel (the Arch-Angel linked with the moon) was the announcing angel, and that the holy grail, as the cup of the last supper, remains popular in fiction and film.

In esotericism part of the journey of the initiate has to be to seek the Grail within, to attain it in the Quest Perilous facing the darkness and monsters inside, to attain mastery over elements within, and aim to eventually walk in peace on the sunlit shores of their own conscience towards knowledge and conversation with their own Holy Guardian Angel.

We can work with these images in pathworkings and meditation, in ritual and trancework. On a practical level we can find peace and regeneration walking by the sea and gazing at the moon. A good experiment while keeping a magical diary is to keep a tide-table as well as noting the planetary movements, especially if you are working with water energies of whatever ilk.

We can also build on the work that has been done by our magical predecessors. We can all learn from Fortune's fictional Wilfred as he gazes at the moon night after night, and enters into to communion with her. We can all learn from the mysterious Morgan as she lights the fire of Azrael - cedar, juniper and sandalwood, upon a wild headland and watches as tide hisses round the flames, and scented sacred fire floats on water, embodying the holy hexagram, that she will later invoke into herself and her priest.

The moon that silvered the world whenever we first noticed it is the same moon that will silver the world when we are long gone, and our earthly bodies have turned to dry dust. When our atoms blend with other atoms in the firmament, infinitely small, the same moon will look down, serene, as She did over the temples of ancient Egypt, and as Artemis stepped softly in the sylvan woods of ancient Greece.

We can all access her door of dreams. There are maps for us to follow in such ancient magic, for there is wisdom to be found in folklore of the dangers of straying too far in a moon-led dance by the nameless shore. The art magical realigns us with the moon, the Great Mother, and with the mysteries of Nature itself. It shows us the hidden doorway from whence we can fly by night to the realms ruled by the moon, and by the other forces that rule the tides great and small; the tides that move the universe, and the tides that ebb and flow within us all.

Selected Bibliography

Crowley, Viviane (2000) *A Woman's Kabbalah. Kabbalah for the 21st Century.* Thorsons.
Endres K.P., and Schad W., (2002/1997) *Moon Rhythms in Nature. How lunar cycles affect living organisms.* Floris Books.
Fortune, Dion, (1935/1987) *The Mystical Qabalah.* The Aquarian Press.
Fortune, Dion, (1935/1989) *The Sea Priestess.* The Aquarian Press.
Fortune, Dion, (1956/2003) *Moon Magic.* Red Wheel/Weiser.
http://www.biodynamics.in/Rhythms.htm
http:/www.ga.water.usg.gov/edu/waterproperties.html
http://www.princeton.edu/~pccm/outreach/scsp/water_on_earth/tides/sciences/causes
http://www.waterinfo.org/resources/water-facts

INDEX

6th and 7th Books of Moses .. 95

A

Achelous 37
Agasou Jemen 53, 61, 62
Agwe 50, 52, 53, 54, 57, 60, 61, 62, 63, 64, 65
Ahuramazda 22
Aida Wedo 54, 58
Aidoneus 68
Aima 167
Ama 167
Anahita .. 10, 20, 21, 22, 23, 24, 25, 26, 27, 28, 29, 30
Aphrodite 42, 45, 152, 155
Apsu 78
Aristides 68
Aristotle 68, 85
Artemis 171
Athena 68
Athenagoras 68
Atlantis 142, 149
Azriel of Gerona 79

B

Bacabs 132
Baron Samedi 51, 52
Belisama 37
Bibi Shahr Banoo 26
Binah 144, 147, 167
Boann 37
Boyne 37
Braint 37
Bran the Blessed 39
Brent 37

Bride 88, 89, 90, 91, 92, 93, 94
Brigantia 37
Brighid 26

C

Chac 132, 133, 134
Chac Xib Chac 132
Charybdis 153
Chokmah 167
Clota 37
Clyde 37
Coventina 153
Crocell 101
Cronos 42

D

Damballah Wedo 54, 58
Dee 37
Demeter 68
Deva 37
Diana 115
Dindshenchas 37, 87
Diodorus Siculus 39
Dion Fortune 11, 141, 143, 144, 145, 146, 147, 165, 167
Donar Water 120, 121

E

Ek Xib Chac 132
Empedocles 67, 68
Erzulie Freda 53
Eusebius 68
Excalibur 36, 109, 111, 112, 116, 155, 170

F

Faery . 110, 111, 112, 113, 114, 115, 116
Fairy 81
Fire of Azrael 146, 171
Focalor 101

G

Gabriel. 78, 124, 136, 139, 140, 170
Gaia 42, 147
Ganga 31
Ganges 31, 37, 86, 164
Général Dessalines 63
Ghede 51
Ginen 49, 50, 51, 56, 57
Gnostic Mass 135, 137, 138, 139
Goetia 10, 101
Gran Aloumba 65
Gran Bwa 51
Gran Simba 65
Grimoire of Pope Honorius 96
Grindylow 39, 123
Gwyn ap Nudd 37

H

Haagenti 101
Hafren 37
Hecate 115
Hephaestus 68
Heptameron 96
Hera 68, 152
Heraclitus 79, 80
Hermes 109, 115
Holy Spirit 97, 139
Horus 135, 136

I

Imammou 52, 53, 60
Isis 68, 116, 122, 144, 145, 147

J

Jenny Greenteeth 123
Jesus 115, 136, 139
Josephus 68
Jumna 37

K

Kabbalah 166
Kan Xib Chac 132
Kelpie 39, 41, 149
Key of Solomon .. 69, 79, 96, 97, 98, 99, 100, 101, 104, 105, 150, 151
Klemezine Klemey 53, 64
Kraken 149

L

La Baleine 53, 58
La Sirene 53, 56, 57, 58, 61
Legba 60
Lemegeton 101
Leonardo Da Vinci 84
Levanah 165
Loch Ness Monster 149, 155
Lourdes 164
Lucifer 115, 116
Lumiel .... 115, *See* Lucifer
Luna 165

M

Maman Brigitte 51
Mambo La Sirene 52, 56
Mambo Lovanah 65
Manetho 68
Meander 37

Melusine 81
Mercury 60, 77, 78, 99, 109
Merlin 109, 110, 111, 113, 114, 115, 116, 117, 119
Mermaid 11, 42, 52, 54, 56, 57, 76, 128, 149
Met Agwe Tawoyo 52
Mikva 164
Mithra 22, 23, 24, 26, 29
Moon 11, 33, 68, 78, 96, 99, 104, 105, 118, 129, 132, 142, 144, 145, 146, 161, 165, 166, 167, 168, 169, 170, 171

N

Nantosuelta 37
Neck 39
Neg Za Zi 51
Nelly Long-Arms 123
Nereide 149
Nerthus 153
Nestis 68, 78
Niagara Falls 157
Nibelungenlied 36
Nile 68, 79, 86
Nimue .. 10, 109, 110, 111, 112, 113, 114, 115, 116, 117
Noah 95, 151
Nodens 37
Nudd 37
Nuit 139

O

Oceanus 68
Odin 109
Ogou Badagris 63
Ogou Balendjo 53, 63, 64
Ogou Batala 63

Ogou Chango 63
Ogou Feray 63
Ogou Yamsan 53, 63, 64
Ogún 128
Olokun 128
Osiris 68
Ossaín 128
Oxún 128

P

Pallas Athene 153
Peg Powler 123
Persephone 78, 165
Philo 68
Philolaos 68, 69
Plato 68, 85
Pliny the Elder 23
Plutarch 23
Poseidon 78, 155
President Klemeille 53

Q

Quitta 49

R

Ra 116, 136
Randolph, Pascal 75
Rhine 35, 36
Ribble 37
Rudra 31

S

Sabrina 37
Sac Xib Chac 132
Sacred Magic of Abramelin the Mage 106
Saint Beuno 38
Saint Brigit 26
Saint Claire 64

Saint Keyne............................ 37
Saint Oswald........................ 37
Saint Thomas Aquinas 85
Scylla.................................. 153
Seine..................................... 37
Selene................................. 165
Selkie............................. 42, 43
Sequana............................... 37
Severn 37
Shannon............................... 86
Shiva.................................... 31
Silibo 53, 61, 62
Simbi Andezo 60
Simbi Anpaka 60
Simbi Dlo............................. 60
Simbi Ganga 60
Simbi Makaya 60
Siren............... 11, 42, 43, 128
Skeleton Woman 45
St Winifreds 164
Sulis 39, 153
Sun....................................... 68
Sword of Moses 95, 97, 103
Sworn Book of Honorius........ 97

T

Tacitus............................... 153
Tatha 37
Tay 37
Thales of Miletius................. 78
Thames................................ 35

The Sea Priestess. 11, 141, 144, 145, 147, 165
Thoth 109, 135, 136, 144
Tiamat.................................. 78

U

Undine 78, 80, 81, 149
Uranus................................. 42

V

Vaga..................................... 37
Venus................22, 33, 44, 132
Vepar.................................. 101
Verbeia................................. 37
Vine.................................... 101

W

Wharfe................................. 37
Wye 37

Y

Yemanyá.. 10, 18, 57, 125, 126, 127, 128, 129, 130, 163
Yesod..........................166, 167

Z

Zagan 102
Zambezi............................. 125
Zeus 68, 153
Zoroaster....................... 21, 80
Zosimos of Panopolis 69

OTHER WORKS BY KIM HUGGENS

Books:

Sol Invictus: The God Tarot deck and book set. Schiffer Books, Ltd, 2008. Co-authored with Nic Phillips.

Tarot 101: Mastering the Art of Reading the Cards, Llewellyn Publications, Spring 2010.

Anthologies:

Between Gods and Men: the nature of daimons in Graeco-Roman literature, theology, and magic in *Both Sides of Heaven*, edited by Sorita d'Este, 2009.

Silent Priestesses: Women of power in early Christianity in *Priestesses, Pythonesses and Sibyls*, edited by Sorita d'Este, 2008.

The Horns of Cattle on the Head of a God – Veles in Slavic Myth in *Horns of Power*, edited by Sorita d'Este, 2007.

The Mithras Liturgy: cult liturgy, religious ritual, or magical theurgy? Some aspects and considerations of the Mithras Liturgy from the Paris Codex and what they may imply for the origin and purpose of this spell in *The Mithras Reader*, vol. 2, edited by Payam Nabarz, 2008.